WHERE IS ALBERTA'S WEALTH GOING?

Follow the Money

WHERE IS ALBERTA'S WEALTH GOING?

Follow the Money

KEVIN TAFT with Mel McMillan and Junaid Jahangir

DETSELIG ENTERPRISES LIMITED
Calgary

5 4 3 2 1

Published by
Detselig Enterprises Ltd.
210 1220 Kensington Road NW
Calgary, Alberta T2N 3P5

www.temerondetselig. com
sales@temerondetselig.com

ISBN 978-1-55059-435-5

Library and Archives Canada Cataloguing in Publication
Taft, Kevin, 1955–
          Follow the money : where is Alberta's wealth
going? / Kevin Taft with Mel McMillan and Junaid Jahangir.

ISBN 978-1-55059-435-5

          1. Alberta—Appropriations and expenditures.
2. Government spending policy—Alberta.
3. Expenditures, Public—Alberta. I. McMillan, Melville L.
II. Jahangir, Junaid III. Title.

HJ7664.A4T34 2012   336.3'9097123   C2012-900188-0

AUTHOR'S ACKNOWLEDGEMENTS AND DISCLAIMER

This project would not have been possible without the wise counsel of Professor Mel McMillan and the unrelenting number crunching of Junaid Jahangir, PH.D. Many other people helped out too, some of them immeasurably. To all I offer a hearty thanks. Any errors or mistakes are my responsibility alone. I received no payments to produce this work, and no royalties will be collected.

— Kevin Taft

PUBLISHER'S ACKNOWLEDGEMENTS

The *Follow the Money* project is founded on the independent research of Kevin Taft, Melville McMillan and Junaid Jahangir. The project has been carried out in partnership with the Alberta Federation of Labour, Public Interest Alberta and the United Nurses of Alberta. The publisher gratefully acknowledges their assistance.

Contents

List of Graphs

Where Is the Wealth Going?

As I GEARED UP FOR THE FALL SITTING of Alberta's legislative assembly in October 2009, the stream of papers and issues that ceaselessly flows through a politician's life was reaching flood levels. I had annual reports, auditor-general reports, committee reports and special reports to read. Constituency concerns, media clippings, phone messages and letters all competed for my attention.

On October 22, a day otherwise like most, I sat down to check my email before going to bed. It's a nightly chore, and if I slack off I regret it. My email inbox, like those of many people, can pile up very quickly.

I had intended to do a brief skim — make a few quick replies, flag anything that needed more serious follow-up. Then I spotted an email from Mel McMillan.

A message from Mel
Mel McMillan is an economics professor at the University of Alberta, and a former chair of that department. He specializes in public economics — the study of government policy and its role in the economy — and often makes astute and surprising observations about our provincial government. He has a knack for navigating his way through mountains of numbers and statistics, and for bringing us mere mortals along for the journey. He is scrupulous about avoiding ideology and spin.

Mel had released a study earlier that day, and he emailed me, knowing I would be interested in its findings. He attached the report as a PDF. Published by the Parkland Institute at the University of Alberta, it was titled *Breaking the Myth: Alberta's spending is mediocre at best.*

I started reading it. It was getting late, but I kept reading it. Mel had plunged into an issue that had been troubling me for over a year.

In the wake of the 2008 world economic crisis and the collapse of oil and natural gas prices, Alberta had tightened its fiscal belt. The message from the government was clear: Alberta had overspent throughout the energy boom, and the good times were now over.

"We were at the all-you-can-eat buffet for ten years and Albertans were lined up with us," admonished Lloyd Snelgrove, then president of the Treasury Board. [1]

Messages like this had been so unrelenting that they became accepted as fact. The rhetoric of government overspending seeped into the media, and to both sides of the legislature. It even made its way — I'll admit it — into some of my own speeches. I should have been more careful.

There are always voices claiming that governments spend too much, no matter what the situation. Every once in a while, those voices are joined by enough others to form a chorus that drowns out broader debate and overpowers the hard evidence.

In politics, perception is reality, and the perception was created that government spending was out of control. That became the reality for political decision-making. But what did the hard evidence say?

As the months had been passing by, I had noticed a discrepancy, and it increasingly bothered me. I just couldn't recall any all-you-can-eat fiscal buffet for Alberta's public services.

There is no doubt that Alberta's government had increased its spending for several years, but a lot of that was just scrambling to keep up with the oil and gas boom. Hundreds of thousands of people moved to Alberta, but — as Ralph Klein once remarked — they didn't bring their schools, roads or hospitals with them. So, public funds were channelled to some impressive new buildings and highways. But these funds often failed to keep up with overheated construction costs and operating expenses.

---

1 Lloyd Snelgrove was quoted by Graham Thomson in "When it comes to the deficit, the gov't plays the blame game: Not everyone was urging the Tories to spend, spend, spend during the boom times," *Edmonton Journal*, November 28, 2009.

Spending was up in contrast to the slash-and-burn budgetary habits of the 1990s. But we hadn't exactly been indulging in an orgy of excess. If anything, Alberta's public services had come out of the boom with very little to show for it.

I tend to give priority to evidence I can actually see, and I had been watching public services in Alberta closely for many years. From Grande Prairie to Medicine Hat, I hadn't seen very many new hospitals. The few new health-care facilities I did see couldn't function properly because they were short of nurses and doctors — for example, the Sheldon Chumir Health Centre in Calgary and the East Edmonton Health Care Centre. There were some nice new highways, but a lot of the roads I drove on were breaking down. My kids' tuitions fees climbed ever higher. Alberta was the only province that didn't fund programs to feed its hungry schoolchildren. My constituency office struggled to help severely handicapped adults survive from month to month on meagre provincial allowances.

As I clicked through Mel's report, it became clear that he had confirmed my misgivings. Alberta's spending wasn't out of line with the rest of the country. Despite soaring energy prices and a booming economy, we spent about the same, per capita, as any other province.

In other words, our government's loud rhetoric about over-indulging its citizens was overblown. They may have intentionally made up their story, or they may have actually believed it themselves. Either way, it wasn't true.

Making numbers talk

Mel McMillan took his data from existing sources, and then used it to draw clear comparisons.

It sounds simple enough, but it's a rare talent. Most of us have neither the time nor the expertise to dig into the raw numbers, and to sort them into something comprehensible. But the raw numbers are out there, and — as Mel demonstrated — the picture they paint doesn't always match up with what we have been told.

Mel's study was so small he called it a "fact sheet" instead of a report. Whatever he called it, it was tantalizing. His approach could hardly have been more straightforward.

Using data from Statistics Canada, he divided each province's spending by the number of people who lived there. This provided per capita amounts for each province that he could compare with each other: here's what Ontario spent per person, here's what Alberta spent per person, here's what Quebec spent per person, and so on.

The study's power came from its combination of simple clarity and surprising results. Mel's small fact sheet showed that Alberta's spending on total combined provincial and municipal services ranked from third to sixth among the ten provinces from 2000–01 to 2008–09 — hardly what the government and others, such as the Wildrose Alliance and the Fraser Institute, were claiming.

When examined in more detail, spending on education was relatively high, consistently ranking at or near the top. Spending on social services was in the middle of the pack of provinces. The real surprise was spending on health care. On page 7, I read: "Over the nine years, Alberta's health spending has averaged about eighth spot — that is, the third lowest among the provinces." That explains those persistently overcrowded hospitals, though the government would go into loud denial.

Mel and I and many others know that, with this kind of information, the devil is in the details. Maybe Alberta's spending on health care is lower because we have a younger population with fewer diseases, not because we have a misguided government. On the other hand, maybe Alberta's spending on education isn't as generous as it appears because, with a younger population, we have to spread that money among proportionately more children.

We must be cautious. But we must also be outspoken when we have good information.

The money trail

After I closed my computer for the night, I lay awake wondering about the surprises a bigger study might hold.

If the government hadn't overspent, then where was Alberta's wealth — our money — going?

Because Alberta is rich. Mind-bogglingly rich.

Albertans, through their provincial government, own some of the biggest and most valuable natural resources on earth. Our provincial government is the trustee of that wealth. Through the Alberta legislature, we entrust our government with the huge responsibility of managing our natural resource wealth on our behalf.

A WORD ABOUT THE NUMBERS

Most figures in this book are based on the CANSIM and Financial Management System (FMS) databases of Statistics Canada. At the time of this analysis, these covered the years from 1988–89 to 2008–09.

Here's why CANSIM and FMS are so valuable. Each provincial government reports its revenues and expenditures using different accounting approaches and categories, and these change as the years pass. Governments often announce the same funding several times, or quietly cancel or delay budgeted spending. Government departments are created and dissolved, program names and mandates change, and financial deals with other partners come and go. Governments, opposition parties, interest groups and lobbyists each have agendas, and media reports can be confusing.

To slice through this fog and allow comparisons across provinces and through the years, Statistics Canada sorts and compiles information from every province and territory into standard categories and publishes them in the CANSIM and FMS databases. CANSIM and FMS are two of Statistics Canada's real gems, the best tools we have for drawing comparisons across different provinces.

We supplemented Statistics Canada's numbers with some other standard information, such as statistics from the Canadian Institute for Health Information (CIHI). We picked the most solid sources available, so that we could absolutely trust the answers that we found.

The graphs in this book come from this information — which we also present as tables of data at the back of this book, so you can check out the details for yourself.

The numbers in this book are as straightforward and spin-free as statistics on this topic can get.

On the government's watch, many billions of barrels of our oil, and trillions of cubic feet of our natural gas, have already been extracted, refined, sold and consumed. Amazingly, even with the pace of development increasing every year, we have enough in reserve to last many decades into the future.

So, if the Alberta government is rich, why doesn't it *feel* rich? Why does so much debate in the legislature and in the media centre on cutbacks and scarcity, not investment and prosperity? Why are we so short of hospitals, why are we laying off teachers, and why isn't our provincial savings plan — the Heritage Savings Trust Fund — worth more?

Within days, I approached Mel with the idea of widening the scope of his investigations. Mel enlisted the help of Junaid Jahangir, a Ph.D. candidate in economics. Over the next few months, with Mel's advice on method, Junaid's heavy lifting at the computer, and my bird-dogging the scent that led from question to answer, to another question and another answer, we went hunting through the data.

The hunt led us down a trail of clues and discoveries, with twists and turns and surprises.

And numbers. Lots of numbers that tell compelling stories.

When we finally stopped, months later, our findings went beyond anything I expected. I learned that much of what the government says simply isn't supported by evidence — no surprise there — but I was amazed at the extent and scale of the misinformation and misconceptions. I also came away questioning some of my own basic assumptions — always a healthy exercise.

2

The Stunning Wealth at Stake

ALBERTA IS THE GREAT RAGS TO RICHES story of Confederation. For decades after it was formed in 1905, Alberta was the poor cousin of the west, overshadowed by Manitoba and its big city of Winnipeg, and left behind by Saskatchewan's wheat boom and British Columbia's lumber, mining and seaport economy. In 1936, Alberta hit bottom, becoming the only Canadian province to ever default on its debt.

Today, a single lifetime later, Alberta is the wealthiest province in Canada — and one of the wealthiest jurisdictions in the world. The transformation came with the development of our oil and gas resources, in three great waves. The first wave ran from 1947 to the early 1980s, with the discovery of large fields of conventional oil. The second wave was driven by a natural gas boom that peaked in the 1990s and 2000s, when prices surged and new pipelines carried Alberta's gas to lucrative markets in the U.S. The third wave, the full-scale development of the oil sands, dominated the 2000s and may last for decades.

Alberta has many wonderful assets: its people, forests, land, water and culture. But what sets Alberta apart is its oil and gas wealth.

Just how rich is Alberta?

If the Alberta government listed its oil and gas reserves in its financial statements, we — as the owners of those reserves — would have a better sense of our collective wealth, and probably a more urgent worry about why it has gone missing. But our government does not provide any such accounting in its financial notes.

So, let's do some accounting.

Alberta's oil sands represent the second-largest oil reserve in the world, after Saudi Arabia. To that, we can add the rest of Alberta's petroleum — its conventional oil and natural gas.

Now, divide that resource by Alberta's population — which, after all, isn't that large. We might think of Edmonton and Calgary as big cities, but if you put them together, and then throw in the rest of Alberta, you end up with a population about the size of greater Montreal or metropolitan Seattle. That's it. That small population owns the second-largest energy reserves in the world. To put it starkly, if metro Seattle owned outright the second-largest oil reserve in the world, would you expect it to have deficits, potholes, tuition increases and teacher lay-offs?

At just five dollars a barrel[2], our proven resources alone — that's proven resources, recoverable with current technology — would tally about $890 billion dollars.[3] To get a sense of scale, $890 billion would pay for the entire Alberta government budget in 2011 about twenty-five times over. And there's a lot more out there.

Of course, we can't cash in Alberta's oil and gas all at once, and it wouldn't be sensible even if we could. It has to be pulled from the ground, upgraded and refined, all of which takes huge investments. But the wealth is there, under our very feet.

And that's just the wealth we have in reserve. That doesn't take into account the countless billions of dollars worth of oil and gas Alberta has already produced throughout the decades, and continues to produce today.

---

2   The five-dollar price is just for illustration, and deliberately low to reflect that the oil and gas lie undeveloped in the ground and must be discounted for future use. Imperial Oil lists the value of its proved reserves at $12.66/barrel, discounted at ten percent. See its December 31, 2010, revised filing NI 51-101.

3   The Alberta Department of Energy's 2009–10 annual report lists 170 billion barrels of currently recoverable oil in the oil sands, 1.5 billion in conventional reserves, and 6.5 billion barrels of oil equivalent in established natural gas reserves.

GRAPH 1. GDP PER CAPITA (2009$)

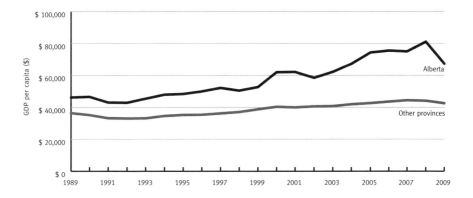

Alberta has a super-sized economy, as this graph shows. When you divide Alberta's economy by its population, Alberta's economy is far bigger per person (or per capita) than the Canadian average. In 2009, it generated $24,740 more per person than the Canadian average — and that was after *the global economic crisis hit.*

Alberta's super-sized economy

As a result of all that wealth, what do we have? Well, for a population our size we have a really big economy.

GDP — gross domestic product — is the standard way to measure an economy. It represents the total value of economic activity in an area at a given time. In general, the bigger the GDP, the richer the area.

Look at Graph 1. It uses Statistics Canada numbers to compare Alberta's economy with the rest of Canada. The lower line on this graph represents the GDP per person per year for all the provinces in Canada *except* Alberta, over a twenty-one-year period, expressed in 2009 dollars. The graph takes us from 1989, on the left, to 2009 on the right. The line shows a gradual increase, from $36,438 per person in 1989 to $44,121 in 2008, with a slight drop to $42,599 in 2009, after the global financial crisis. That line represents the trend in overall economic activity in Canada, outside of Alberta.

Now look at the upper line. It shows Alberta's GDP per person. It is easy to see that Alberta's economy has been consistently larger than the rest of Canada's throughout that period. And, as the years go by, the gap grew and grew, until 2008. By 2008, the per-capita GDP for the rest of Canada was $44,121, while in Alberta it had risen to $81,121. This means that in 2008, Alberta's economy was $37,000 larger per person than the rest of Canada's. For a family of four, that was $148,000 more economic activity in Alberta than in the other provinces.

The gap narrowed following the 2008 global financial crisis, but our province still maintained a huge advantage. And, from early indications, the drop in 2009 was likely a temporary anomaly. The government is already preparing for GDP to resume rapid growth, and is predicting labour shortages over the next ten years. [4]

Let's look at the strength of Alberta's economy from a different angle: the size of provincial government debt. In Graph 2, the upper line shows the provincial government debt for all the provinces other than Alberta. Per capita, adjusted for inflation, it starts at $6,190 of debt. It climbs for a while in the mid-1990s, an era when the federal government was downloading many programs onto the provinces. Finally, debt levels began to trail off a bit by the year 2000.

With Alberta's line, the contrast is obvious. Alberta's debt was climbing, hitting a peak around 1994, and then it shrank very rapidly. At the point where it crosses the horizontal line marked "zero dollars" (0$), Alberta's provincial debt turned into provincial savings.

This is an example of how numbers tell a story. In Alberta's case, the story is of the Klein government's pay-down of Alberta's debt — and it's worth giving some credit where credit is due. The Klein government had a clear plan with a clear goal, and they stuck with it. At the same time, they never paused to ask: at what point does paying down debt compromise the future? They cut health-care spending, and now many Albertans can't find a family doctor. So, here's a note for future rounds of debt reduction: if we pay down debt by cutting, for example, spending on education, our children may not have the knowledge and skills they need as adults. It's like bequeathing a house to your kids that's mortgage free, but with a leaking roof, frayed wiring, and a furnace that no longer works.

It is worth noting that while the Stelmach government ran annual deficits starting in 2008, it did not return the Alberta government to a debt situation. Instead, it drew down its savings by spending from its Sustainability Fund. So, although the Alberta government ran annual

---

4   See comments by Thomas Lukaszuk, then Alberta's employment minister, in
     " 'Severe worker shortages' forecast for Alberta: Some sectors facing crunch already,"
     Calgary Herald, June 12, 2011.

GRAPH 2. GOVERNMENT DEBT PER CAPITA (2009$)

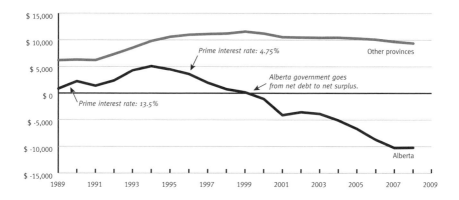

The power of Alberta's super-sized economy shows in this graph, which describes Alberta's debt status compared to the rest of Canada. (The CANSIM data available for this graph ended in 2008.) Alberta's strong economy has kept Alberta's debt consistently low over the last twenty years. In fact, between 2000 and 2008, Alberta's economy generated a big surplus — it paid Alberta's bills and much more.

deficits in response to the global recession that began in 2008, Alberta remains without a net debt.

Alberta's "tiger" economy

When you combine Alberta's GDP growth with its debt-free status, it's clear that we have a very, very powerful economy. In fact, it's the kind of economy that attracts attention from banks around the world — including Canada's own TD Bank.

In September 2007, TD Economics issued its third report in five years on Alberta's booming economy. Titled *The Tiger That Roared Across Alberta*, the report provided an update to earlier reports from 2003 and 2005. All three reports described amazing economic growth in the Calgary–Edmonton corridor. [5]

---

5   TD Economics is part of the TD Bank Financial Group. Here are the titles of the reports, and — where appropriate — the pages quoted from them in this section:
    The Calgary-Edmonton Corridor: Take Action Now To Ensure Tiger's Roar Doesn't Fade, Special Report, April 22, 2003. (Not quoted.)
    An Update on the Economy of the Calgary-Edmonton Corridor: More Action Needed for the Tiger to Roar, Topic Paper, October 3, 2005. Pages 2 and 3 quoted.
    The Tiger That Roared Across Alberta, Special Report, September 27, 2007. Page i and page 2 quoted.

"We thought we were bold," the authors wrote, "when in 2003 we forecast growth in the corridor of 4 percent per year over the 2002–06 period. Yet the actual figure was even more impressive, at 5 percent per year."

I appreciated these reports. Not only were they filled with good information and analysis, they had an honesty and balance that was generally missing from government reports. They conveyed optimism without boosterism.

As I thumbed through the report, its eye-popping numbers just kept jumping out at me. It certainly confirmed that Alberta was prosperous. The Calgary-Edmonton corridor, it said, enjoyed a US$15,000 advantage in GDP per person over the United States. In fact, GDP per capita in Alberta was larger than every country in the world except Luxembourg.

In both its 2005 and 2007 reports, TD Economics calculated the percentage of Alberta's GDP that went to corporate profits. It's not a common calculation. But for a bank it's a sensible marker of the profitability of the private sector.

The 2005 report stated, "Corporate profits grew 44 percent in Alberta... in 2003 and a further 19 percent in 2004. This growth brings corporate profits to 22 percent of Alberta's nominal GDP, roughly twice the share posted in the rest of Canada."

The 2007 report made the same point, showing that corporate profits as a share of Alberta's GDP were 22.8 percent, compared to 12.2 percent in the rest of Canada. Curiously, this particular information stuck in a corner of my mind, sitting alone and unused until, like a missing piece of a jigsaw puzzle, I clicked it into place years later to complete a picture.

In the spirit of due diligence that investors expect, TD Economics didn't shy away from raising concerns, too. Some were obvious: Alberta's economy depended too much on oil and gas, and housing costs were too high. High school drop-out rates were a serious disappointment, and quickly rising tuition fees were making post-secondary education less affordable.

The 2005 report had startled me with the information that 42 percent of individuals living in Calgary were low-income, living on less than $20,000 per year. Income inequality in Calgary was so pronounced that Calgary had both a larger portion of high-income earners and a larger portion of low-income earners than other Canadian cities.

But, overall, the reports were unquestionably enthusiastic about Alberta's prosperity. Of course, I knew how my colleagues across the floor in the legislature would interpret all of this: "Look at how prosperous our great province is. Aren't we doing a fantastic job?" With numbers like these, you could hardly blame them for feeling a bit smug.

Alberta faces challenges no doubt, but they are the challenges of enormous prosperity. And, given the right approach, we have all the tools we need to meet them.

The core message from TD Economics could not be more clear: taken as a whole, Alberta really is mind-bogglingly rich.

3

The Big Picture Evidence on Government Spending

IF YOU DON'T PAY CLOSE ATTENTION — and how many people do? — you'd think the Alberta government was the last of the big-time spenders. In a typical opinion piece on August 17, 2011, called "Alberta's mess of its own making," the *National Post* shouted about the need for Alberta to "rein in" its "wild spending."

The spending-too-much message is a simple and powerful message and I've fallen for it myself, even when it's not supported by the evidence.

So let's look at the evidence.

Some graphic truth about government spending

Graph 3 shows the Alberta government's total spending, per capita in 2009 dollars, compared with the average levels of spending by the other provinces. Again, it covers the twenty-one-year period from 1989 to 2009.

GRAPH 3. TOTAL GOVERNMENT EXPENDITURE PER CAPITA (2009$)

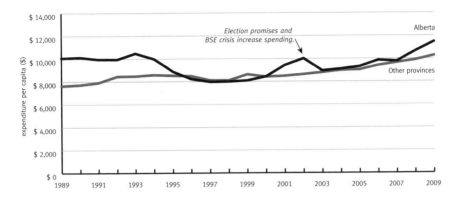

Government spending in Alberta — measured per capita (average per person) — has been near the Canadian average for most of the last fifteen years. The evidence of this graph shows that the Alberta government's record of spending is not out of line with other provinces.

In 1989, the Alberta government was spending well above the average of the other provinces. This shouldn't be surprising, given Alberta's relative wealth. Albertans enjoyed some of the best education, health care, and public benefits in the country. Taxes were low, and there were huge private-sector subsidies. Roads and public buildings were in excellent repair, which proved to be fortunate, given the fate that soon awaited maintenance and construction budgets.

But two big problems arose simultaneously, which led to a third.

BUST FOR DON GETTY

The first was the collapse of oil prices, in the winter of 1986. They fell off a cliff. Through the first half of the 1980s, Alberta's oil sold in the range of US$28 to US$35 a barrel, which was a lot of money in those days. Then, in the winter of 1986, the price dropped to $15, and by summer it hit a low of $11. Don Getty had become premier the previous fall, just in time to watch his government's treasury get decimated. A similar problem became Ed Stelmach's destiny twenty years later. Lucky for him, though, the next problem did not.[6]

---

6   There are many ways to track historical oil prices. I used an internet source: www.indexmundi.com.

The next problem was very high interest rates, which had been ratcheted up by central banks around the world, including the Bank of Canada, to dampen inflation. CANSIM data show that the prime rate in 1988 and 1989 was around 10 to 12 percent, and that in 1990 it passed 13 percent, breaking through 14 percent for a brief time. Mortgage rates and business loans were two or three points higher, or more.

It's easy to forget the impact of high interest rates. At four percent, a ten-year bond of one thousand dollars will cost a government less than five hundred dollars in total interest. At fourteen percent, the same one-thousand-dollar bond will cost a government close to three *thousand* dollars in interest.

So the third problem was inevitable: debt. The Alberta government borrowed heavily to offset the loss of oil revenues. At high interest rates, this borrowing created an accelerating spiral of annual deficits and accumulated debt. Alberta's net debt soared, from almost nothing in 1989, to more than $5,000 per capita in 1994. But even at its peak, Alberta's per-capita debt was only about half the average of the other provinces. (See Table 2 in the back of this book).

Now look again at Graph 3, which shows total spending per capita after adjusting for inflation. From 1989 to 1994, there was no increase in total spending. Despite the image that seems imprinted on the minds of Albertans who lived through Don Getty's time as premier, his government held the line on total spending. In fact, many public programs were cut, including grants to schools and hospitals, in part to allow significant government support of the corporate sector.

We now have the evidence to debunk a myth that grips Alberta to this day, and gets in the way of good government decision-making. It wasn't rapidly increasing public spending that drove Alberta into debt. It was the collapse of oil prices and the brutal rise in interest rates.

BOOM FOR RALPH KLEIN

If Don Getty spent his whole term as premier contending with an economic ice age, Ralph Klein became premier just as the glaciers melted. Such is the luck of politics in Alberta.

For starters, interest rates dropped precipitously. In December 1993, when Klein first became premier, the prime rate had plummeted to 4.1 percent. While the rate crept up the following year, it soon fell again, generally resting below 5 percent. The cost of borrowing fell sweetly for everyone — reducing burdens on government, reassuring families that they could build homes and buy cars, and stimulating businesses to borrow, invest, grow, and pay taxes.

The price of oil remained depressed, but the price of natural gas doubled from 1992 to 1994. It was a sign of the gas boom to come — profits, jobs, royalties and all.

Prosperity returned to Alberta, but some of the hard lessons of the 1980s had been forgotten. It may be that they were never learned.

Ralph Klein, never one to fret the details of policy or economics, stuck to his self-declared strategy of politics: find a parade and get in front of it.

Lining up to the loud drumbeat of groups, including the official Opposition, he and his government rose to the command to drastically cut public spending. They told the public that Alberta's spending was spiralling out of control, so we had to squeeze until it hurt, and then squeeze some more. In a famous misdiagnosis, provincial treasurer Jim Dinning chanted: "We have a spending problem, not a revenue problem."

It's a misdiagnosis repeated these days by politicians such as Danielle Smith of the Wildrose Alliance and groups such as the Canadian Taxpayers Federation.

But, look back at the evidence in Graph 3. In the five years before the Klein government began its cuts, total spending by the Alberta government was nearly flat. And I have personal knowledge that many people inside the government knew this, including cabinet ministers. Their internal evidence actually showed total program spending had been flat for ten years, since 1983.

Jim Dinning had it backwards. Alberta's deficits and debts weren't caused by soaring public spending. It was revenue that was the problem. The Alberta government had become addicted to oil and gas revenues, but these were wildly erratic. When there was a rush, it was great. But when oil and gas revenues were in short supply, it was a crisis. The real problem was that revenues had fallen, and there was no back-up plan.

Quitting cold turkey was too painful, so the government turned to borrowing, at a time when central banks around the world were charging loan-shark rates. Alberta's fiscal strategies placed our economic fate into the hands of OPEC oil ministers, anyone who wanted to start a fight in the Middle East, and central bankers in foreign capitals.

Unless the Alberta government breaks its fiscal addiction to directly spending oil and gas revenues, we will hit the economic skids again. And, sooner or later, Alberta won't recover.

The Klein government ignored all this. It started cutting public services, and once it started, it went at it hard.

As a result, we can see in Graph 3 that Alberta's spending level fell below the line for the rest of Canada by 1996. For the remainder of the 1990s, we sat in the lower range of all Canadian provinces when it comes to government spending.

But, remember how I said numbers can tell a story? In 2001–02, you can see a sudden upward blip in Alberta's spending. That blip tells another interesting story.

THAT BLIP IN 2001

In 2001, Ralph Klein fought an election campaign against then-Alberta Liberal leader Nancy MacBeth. The two had been bitter rivals since the early 1990s, when they both vied for the leadership of the Progressive Conservatives. Nancy (whose last name at the time was Betkowski) was widely seen to represent the party's "progressive" side, and Klein the "conservative." Shortly after losing the leadership race, she left provincial politics.

MacBeth returned in 1998, this time as leader of the official Opposition. Heading into the 2001 election, she had strong hopes of drawing support from "Red Tories" who had become disaffected by the Klein cuts.

In the lead-up to that election, however, the provincial purse strings miraculously loosened. There were tax cuts and hurried reinvestments in health care, and the government made some very generous labour settlements. A boom in natural gas was pouring revenues into the provincial treasury, allowing the government to announce in September 2000 that it would be mailing $300 to every Albertan aged sixteen and over in two payments during the coming winter.

The voters rewarded him for this strategy. When election day came, Klein and his government won 73 of 84 seats.

So, that sudden blip in spending — a sharp rise in 2001 carrying over into 2002 — tells, in part, the story of the famous Klein-MacBeth grudge match.

BACK WHERE WE STARTED

By 2003, the blip was over. Since then, Alberta's total spending on programs in most years has remained close to the Canadian average — and, in real terms, its spending is not a whole lot more than it was way back in 1989.

We've ended up pretty much back where we started, after a long and disruptive journey.

Wild gyrations in spending tend to be inefficient and counter-productive. Alberta's spending patterns have tended to swing between feast and famine, with program cuts, layoffs, deferred maintenance, and project postponements followed by expansions, hiring drives, and capital splurges. This is a poor way to manage public services.

Start-stop driving is hard on your gas mileage, and the same holds true for governments.

Fact: A Shrinking Share of Wealth for Public Services

AFTER ALL THE UPS AND DOWNS, THE Alberta government's spending per capita, adjusting for inflation, isn't a whole lot different now than it was in 1989: the five-year average for 2005–09 is $10,208, and the five-year average for 1989–93 is $10,119. (See Table 3 in the back of this book.)

But, remember what happened to Alberta's economy during that same period? It grew dramatically, far more than population growth and inflation. About 70 percent more.

In other words, while Alberta's economy soared over those two decades, per capita provincial spending stalled.

The picture shifted somewhat in 2009, after the global financial crisis. Alberta's GDP shrank, which drove up — in relative terms — the percentage of GDP represented by government spending. Even so, government spending remained a small portion of the economy. And, again, indications suggest that the economic slowdown in Alberta in 2008 was an anomaly.

This means that over the past two decades, government spending became smaller and smaller as a portion of the economy. The same has happened for Canada as a whole, but as Graph 4 shows, in Alberta the drop has been much more.

GRAPH 4. TOTAL GOVERNMENT EXPENDITURE AS A PERCENTAGE OF GDP (2009$)

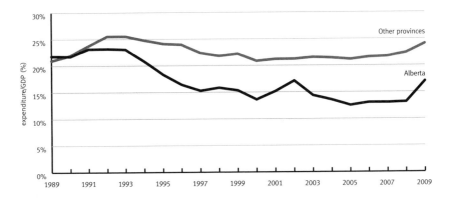

Government spending in Alberta has been well below the Canadian average when you measure it as a percentage of GDP. GDP describes the total value of an economy at any point in time. This graph answers the question: from year to year, what portion of that total value did government spending represent in Alberta and in Canada? The graph shows that total government spending in Alberta is trending down.

As a society, Alberta spent a steadily shrinking portion of its increasing prosperity on provincial public services. For the five years from 1989 to 1993, Alberta government spending averaged 23 percent of GDP. For the five years from 2005 to 2009, it averaged 14 percent of GDP. This represents a downsizing by more than a third of the provincial government as a portion of Alberta's economy. (See Table 4 in the back of this book.)

But how did government spending look sector by sector? Maybe spending was out of control in health care or education.

To be thorough — and cautious — we tracked down more evidence.

Numbers as Evidence

WE'RE GOING TO EXAMINE THE PRIME suspect for government over-spending — health care — in the next chapter.

But before we get there, here's a quick primer on numbers. We're going to walk through some numbers on health care to show you how they work.

Because you have to watch out for numbers.

Numbers can be twisted out of shape, and the twisted graphs and charts they make can be surprisingly convincing.

Example Graph 1, next page, shows the Alberta government's spending on health care from data straight out of Statistics Canada.

This graph is enough to make a taxpayer weak in the knees. Alberta's spending on health care starts out in 1989 at about $4 billion, and ends up twenty-one years later at $12 billion. That's triple the expenditure in just two short decades.

When we look at this graph, we automatically picture the line continuing up and up into the future. How much will we spend on health care twenty years from today? Will that $12 billion triple again?

Given graphs like this one, it's no surprise that the rhetoric has skyrocketed. Eventually, health care will take up the entire provincial budget! We won't have any money left for other government programs! If we don't rein in these costs — and soon — we're all doomed!

EXAMPLE GRAPH 1. ALBERTA'S SPENDING ON HEALTH CARE, UNADJUSTED

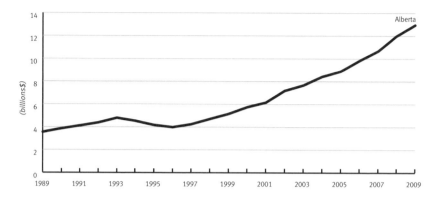

This line is steep — and misleading.

It's easy to find think-tank reports and media stories that demand cuts to health care in the name of sustainable spending — for example, *Canada's Medicare Bubble* from the Fraser Institute in April 2011, or the editorial "Canada's 6-percent health-care fetish" in the *Globe and Mail* on April 26, 2011. Maybe these reports and stories are working with graphs like Example Graph 1.

Because, there are two very big problems with this graph.

PROBLEM 1: ADJUSTING FOR INFLATION

First, the graph doesn't adjust for inflation. To get a sense of the impact of inflation, take your wallet on this quick trip down memory lane:

- In 1988, the average residential selling price in Calgary was $99,000; twenty years later it passed $500,000.
- In 1988, one-year tuition for a full-time student seeking a B.A. at the University of Alberta was $995; twenty years later it was $4,900.
- In July, 1988, crude oil traded for US$15.50 a barrel, and a litre of gasoline was about 50 cents.

In short, twenty years ago, dollars were worth much more than they are today. If you don't account for this change, you will not have valid information.

So let's adjust the Alberta government's spending for inflation and take a fresh look at the numbers in Example Graph 2.

EXAMPLE GRAPH 2. ALBERTA'S SPENDING ON HEALTH CARE, ADJUSTED FOR INFLATION

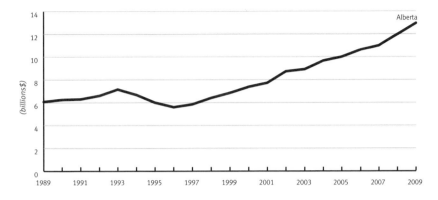

Compare this line with the line in Example Graph 1: it's less steep. But it's still misleading.

To remove the effects of inflation, we have now adjusted all the figures to reflect values in constant 2009 dollars.

Once we convert everything to 2009 dollars, the province spent about $6 billion in 1989 and about $13 billion in 2009.

That scary, skyrocketing line in the first graph has now started to flatten out. It now shows that health-card spending has doubled, not tripled.

But a doubling of costs is still pretty serious. That line isn't quite as steep anymore, but it's still awfully daunting. And it's still seriously misleading.

PROBLEM 2: ADJUSTING FOR A GROWING POPULATION

A second big problem remains with Example Graph 2: we haven't adjusted it for Alberta's larger population.

In 1989, there were 2.4 million people in Alberta. By 2009 there were 3.7 million. Those extra 1.3 million people meant the population had increased by 50 percent in twenty years. Those people worked hard, raised families, and filled jobs for eager employers, which is why most of them moved to Alberta in the first place. They also paid taxes, and used public services such as health care. So, of course, the Alberta government was spending more money, just like the government of

EXAMPLE GRAPH 3. ALBERTA'S SPENDING ON HEALTH CARE, ADJUSTED FOR INFLATION AND POPULATION

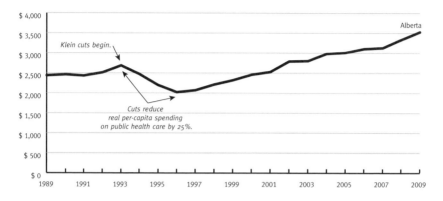

This line — the least steep of the three — also presents the most valid information of the three.

New York spends more money than the government of New Sarepta. Size matters.

When you adjust for population growth as well as inflation, the skyrocketing line in Example Graph 1 flattens out even more. You can see this in Example Graph 3. Now the line starts at around $2,400, jogs up and down over the years (reflecting our government's erratic budgeting) and ends up at about $3,500. In sum, the Alberta government's spending on health care rose $1,100 per person from 1989 to 2009, after accounting for inflation and population growth.

It's enough of an increase to spark some discussion. But let's put this in perspective: this is a rise of 1.9 percent compounded per year over twenty-one years. That hardly merits terms like "skyrocketing" or "out of control." That would be like reading your bank statement and saying, "Yikes, look at my savings account — that 1.9 percent interest rate is out of control!"

All three of these health-care graphs present accurate data, but accuracy is not always the same as truth. As I said, you have to watch out for numbers.

By accounting for the effects of inflation and population, we can more easily (and accurately) examine the actual trends over time. If you flip back a few pages to the graphs on provincial GDP, debt and total government expenditures, you'll see that we have already been doing this.

Throughout this book, unless it is noted otherwise, the graphs are presented using per capita data, in 2009 dollars. Junaid did a lot of work to make this possible — gathering the numbers, entering them into simple spreadsheets, and adjusting them for inflation and population. (We have made many of the spreadsheets into the tables at the back of this book, for those of you who share our passion for spreadsheets).

THE GAZE OF THE PYTHON

"Hold spending increases on public services to inflation and population growth." That's a refrain often repeated by politicians such as Ted Morton, during his run for the Tory leadership, and Danielle Smith, leader of the Wildrose Alliance.

It's a tempting idea — tempting, like the gaze of a python.

Holding public sector spending to the rates of inflation and population growth actually puts public services in a long-term death squeeze.

Growth in our economy is what happens over and above inflation and population increases. It's this growth that means we have a higher standard of living than our grandparents. Freezing public services out of that growth means public services cannot keep pace with changes in the rest of society.

Let's imagine a government had imposed this policy in, say, 1971. We'd be trying to run a government today on a financial base of forty years ago. Government regulators with computers? Sorry, not with a budget based on pencils and slide rules. Twinned highways with overpasses? Be happy with single lanes and stop signs. Heart transplants? You've got to be kidding. Of course, no public servants would be around to answer these questions — who wants to work in 2011 for the standard of living of 1971?

A public sector run on a budget frozen to inflation and population growth would soon become a drag on the economy. Services we need — everything from environmental regulation to universities to bridges — would get left further and further behind improvements in the rest of the economy.

6

The Prime Suspect: Health Care

IT'S EASY TO GET LOST IN THIS MYSTERY about government spending and the fate of public wealth. The biggest place to get lost is health care spending, and not only because it has the biggest numbers. It also has life-and-death impact, and it is caught in an ideological, political, and economic tussle over private versus public delivery.

The angry debate and accusations make health care an especially difficult sector to navigate. So, it's important to take our bearings carefully, using the best evidence available.

Taking a first bearing: per capita spending

You've already seen the basic trends on Alberta's health-care spending in the previous chapter about numbers as evidence. When you adjust for inflation and population growth, there's an increase in spending for sure, but hardly an alarming one.

So, our first bearing on Alberta's provincial health care spending comes from Statistics Canada's CANSIM database, one of the most reliable around.

Junaid also ran the same CANSIM data for the other provinces. The results are in Graph 5. This graph shows the amount, per capita, in 2009 dollars, that Canada's other provincial governments spent on health care, compared to Alberta's government.

GRAPH 5. HEALTH-CARE EXPENDITURE PER CAPITA (2009$)

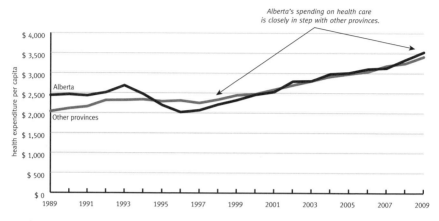

Of all the sectors where government overspending might be an issue in Alberta, health care is the top of the list. But, between 1995 and 2000, Alberta's government spent below the Canadian average. Since 2001, its spending has been at par.

Again, we see Alberta's erratic trends in spending. And, once again, we see the significance of the 1993 general election.

From 1993 to 1996, in Ralph Klein's first few years as premier, Alberta cut its spending on health care by twenty-five percent. (See Table 5 in the back of this book.) If you were in Alberta during those years, you may remember the stories told by those numbers.

More than ten thousand health workers — nurses, technicians, lab staff — lost their jobs. Hundreds of young nursing graduates left Alberta to work in the United States.[7] In Edmonton, hospital wards were mothballed, leaving entire wings of hospitals abandoned. At least those could be reclaimed when the time came. In Calgary the decisions were irreversible: the Holy Cross and Grace hospitals were sold to private companies, and the Calgary General Hospital, one of the largest hospitals in Alberta, was shuttered, then demolished, and its land sold for condos. Calgary has been badly short of hospital beds ever since.

Training programs for doctors, nurses and others were whittled back, further injuring the system. This was the kind of short-term pain that also creates long-term pain, for it soon contributed to a chronic shortage of health professionals in Alberta. By the year 2000, Alberta's

---

7 This damage was documented in a February 1998 report from the Alberta Department of Health called "Health Workforce Adjustment Strategy Project Report."

remaining doctors and nurses were so valued they could demand huge wage settlements from a government desperate to calm its health-care controversies. I watched as health authorities had to pay fat overtime bills and go on expensive international recruiting drives. So much for cost savings and efficiency via dramatic cuts.

The Alberta government's spending on health care hit bottom in 1996, as the line on the graph shows. Junaid's data only goes back to 1988, but my knowledge of earlier Statistics Canada data shows that Alberta's spending on health care in 1996 was the lowest per capita since the 1970s. It simply wasn't enough to sustain a modern health-care system.

By late 1995, the flashpoint came: a wildcat strike by laundry workers at the Calgary Regional Health Authority. Already paid low wages, the laundry workers walked out when they were told their jobs were to be contracted out. The plight of these workers struck a chord with other workers, and with the public. Within days, the threat of much broader walkouts arose. Realizing a limit had been reached, the Klein government backed off.

From 1997 onwards, Alberta's health-care spending has slowly recovered, running parallel to the trend in the rest of Canada. Even though much of this increase has been spent repairing the damage from the mid-1990 cuts, Alberta's health-care system has never fully recovered.

Taking a second bearing: spending as a percentage of GDP

One of the most common ways to measure health-care spending is to look at it as a portion of GDP. This tells us what portion of an overall economy is being spent on health care.

In this case the Alberta government really stands out, not for how much it devotes to health care, but for how little. Since 1994, public spending on health care in Alberta has ranged from around 4 percent to around 5 percent of GDP, as you can see in Graph 6. This is far below the spending rate of other provinces, which consistently averages about 7 percent.

The reason? We are back to Alberta's huge GDP: our economy is so large it makes our spending on health care seem small. Current spending on public health care isn't going to bankrupt Alberta.

GRAPH 6. HEALTH-CARE EXPENDITURE AS A PERCENTAGE OF GDP (2009$)

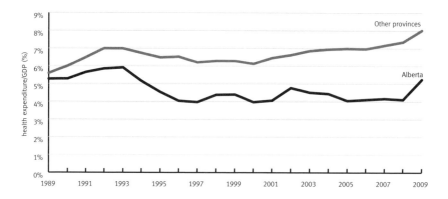

This graph shows that health-care spending by Alberta's government is much lower than the Canadian average, and has slumped over the last twenty years, when measured as a percentage of Alberta's GDP. This is the opposite of what you would expect if health-care spending were out of control.

If you really get into this stuff, here's something interesting: private spending on health care, which is far larger than most Canadians realize, would raise the numbers in Graph 6 by almost half if it were included, lifting the total public and private spending on health care in Canada to about eleven percent of GDP.[8]

Taking a third bearing: the CIHI data

Our first two bearings tell us Alberta's spending on health care is gradually increasing in line with other provinces, but as a portion of our economy it is easily affordable. Just to be sure, let's go for a third bearing, this one from the Canadian Institute for Health Information (CIHI).

CIHI is a national treasure, even though few Canadians know of its existence. A non-profit corporation funded by federal, provincial and territorial governments, CIHI gathers data on health care from coast to coast.

In the words of its vision, CIHI provides "unbiased, credible and comparable information that will enable health leaders to make better-

---

8   *National Health Expenditure Trends, 1975 to 2010,* Canadian Institute for Health Information, October, 2010, pages 2–16.

informed decisions."[9] CIHI data allows us to identify trends over time, and to draw comparisons among different regions of the country. Take my word for it, CIHI produces a *lot* of information on health care in Canada.

CIHI adjusts provincial spending on health care to reflect the different age structures of each province. Spending on health care is affected by the age of a province's population. In general, the higher the portion of elderly people in a population, the greater the need for spending on health care.

Because Alberta has a younger population than other provinces, but spends about the same per capita as other provinces, this measure shows that Alberta effectively spends more on health care, vying with Newfoundland and Labrador for top spot. (See Table 5a in the back of this book.)

So CIHI's age-adjusted calculations for Alberta's health spending are higher in comparison to the unadjusted figures from Statistics Canada.

On October 28, 2010, CIHI released a report: *National Health Expenditure Trends, 1975 to 2010*. This is exactly the kind of report that deserves a few public headlines. It confirmed what many people have been saying for years: health-care costs are rising, but they are by no means soaring out of line.

The report is 155 pages, so let's cut to the chase. Here is a quick list of where the Alberta government's spending on health care stands. It ranks third in spending per capita, behind Newfoundland and Manitoba, and just ahead of Saskatchewan. When CIHI adjusts for Alberta's younger population, our government's spending per person (in 2008) rose to first. When we adjust for Alberta's larger economy, it falls to last in the country.

SOME INTERNATIONAL AMMO

You probably get the idea: depending on your measurement, Alberta's health-care spending can look high, low or mid-range.

For Canada as a whole, CIHI did have a few encouraging surprises. Although health-care costs were still rising, the growth rate had slowed to its lowest point since 1997. As a portion of national GDP, combined

---

9   All of the data in this section on the Canadian Institute for Health Information (CIHI) comes from its report *National Health Expenditure Trends, 1975 to 2010*, October 2010. The pages referenced include: inside cover page, page xi, and pages 33, 39, 57, 62, and 65.

public and private health-care spending had actually declined slightly in 2010 — to 11.7 percent from 11.9 percent.

One big surprise for me came out in the international comparisons. The report pointed out that Canada's per capita spending on health care remains about average for a developed country, and significantly lower than that of the U.S. The big surprise was the portion of private sector health spending in Canada.

The Canadian Taxpayers Federation, and other groups, have over the years made a claim that goes like this: "Canada is the only country in the world outside Cuba and North Korea that bans private health care." It has always been a ridiculous statement, but I didn't realize how ridiculous until I read this CIHI report. Here is the quote from CIHI: "Canada, with private-sector per person spending of US$1,216, is among the top three countries with the highest per capita health spending funded by the private sector." The data is right there: only the U.S. and Switzerland have higher private-sector spending on health care than Canada. A few pages later, the CIHI report shows Canada ranks eighteenth in the developed world — that's right, eighteenth — for the portion of total health spending that comes from the public sector.

There's a big piece of ammo for some myth busting.

I kept an eye on the media for the following few days, to see what kind of play the report would get. To me, it seemed like big news — solid data that shattered some widely held misconceptions. I had a hunch that it wouldn't exactly dominate the front pages. In fact, the report failed to earn any mention at all in either Edmonton daily newspaper. I didn't find it in Calgary's papers, either.

A reality check

The papers in Edmonton and Calgary didn't have space for the CIHI story, but they did have space for another one. Here's the headline from the *Edmonton Journal* on April 14, 2011, during the federal election: "Country should be debating how to pay for health care: Despite warning from Dodge, our electioneering politicians are avoiding the issue."

Former Bank of Canada Governor David Dodge and a colleague, Richard Dion, had released a study called "Chronic Healthcare Spending Disease," published by the C.D. Howe Institute in April 2011. In keeping with the report's provocative title, the *Journal* headline gave the impression that Dodge and Dion felt the end of public health care was near — or ought to be.

But if you went past this hype and read the research itself, the report was almost reassuring. On page 1 it notes that Canada's health-care spending has been rising slowly for thirty-five years, but that economic growth "...has still left plenty of additional income each year to be devoted to consumption of other goods and services, to investment, and to other public services." It goes on to say that if things continue this way over the next two decades "...then there is no reason to think that it would be unsustainable for the share of national income devoted to healthcare to continue to rise..." at the same rate as in the past.

Dodge and Dion do say that governments will be faced with difficult choices, including the possibility of raising taxes, and that the pressure to improve the system will be unrelenting. Fair enough. But it's safe to say that all the responsible data on health-care spending points to a consistent conclusion: health-care spending in Alberta and across Canada is on a gradual long-term upward trend that is well within reason.

Is it cause for panic? No.

Will laying off a few hundred nurses for a year fix anything? No.

Can the Alberta government afford to deliver a first-class public health-care system if it wants to, and like it once did? Absolutely.

Do we need to keep managing the system better? Of course. Good management is more important than juicy budget increases.

7

A Diagnosis of Chronic Crisis

September 2010, Royal Alexandra Hospital, Edmonton. Shane Hay came to the emergency room at the Royal Alex in the middle of the night, desperate for help. He was on the verge of killing himself, he realized, and he needed somebody to prevent him from going through with it.

A thirty-four-year-old patient with bipolar disorder, Hay had checked himself out of the University of Alberta hospital earlier that evening, before taking a long, lonely walk across Edmonton's High Level Bridge.

For most of a year, Hay had struggled with suicidal impulses. Despite medical care and a strongly supportive family, he sometimes felt himself slipping into the kind of depression few of us can even imagine. At those times he was wise enough, and courageous enough, to seek professional intervention.

Nobody will ever know why he walked away from the U of A Hospital that night. But we do know what happened later, when he walked into the Royal Alex.

At the triage desk, Hay told the nurse he was suicidal. Staff led him to a room with a stretcher, and he waited.

Every forty minutes, someone stopped by to check on him, but still he waited. Every hour or so, he emerged to ask for a counsellor, but still he waited.

After twelve agonizing hours, he came out one last time and asked for a pen and paper. He returned to the room. "There's no place for me in the good world," he wrote in a note. He thanked his parents, and apologized for what he was about to do. He then signed, "Your loving son forever."

Using the strap from his backpack, Shayne Hay hanged himself from the light fixture. By the time staff discovered him, it was too late.

The reality of chronic crisis

When *Edmonton Journal* reporter Jodie Sinnema broke the Shayne Hay story on November 13, 2010, she put a vivid, heart-wrenching face on the crisis in Alberta's health-care system.

Because there *is* a chronic crisis in health care in Alberta, but it's *not* a crisis of overspending.

In a province where emergency-room workers are routinely overwhelmed, and where mental-health services are among the weakest and most underfunded in Canada, cases like Shayne Hay's are not uncommon. In a follow-up story, Sinnema listed eleven similar examples of psychiatric patients who died while in care, all within the previous four years. Eleven in four years. Each of these cases has its own set of specific details, as desolate and disturbing as those endured by Shayne Hay.

In the legislature, the government expressed its regret and its condolences, with obvious sincerity, but could offer little in the way of tangible action. Gene Zwozdesky, Alberta's health minister, said "people should take some comfort" in knowing that Alberta's health system was already under review.

By then, emergency-room overcrowding had dominated Alberta's political scene for weeks. The latest uproar had been sparked by a letter from the Alberta Medical Association to Zwozdesky, warning of a possible "catastrophic collapse" of emergency care in Alberta. The letter was backed up with pages of documented examples of substandard care. These examples were supplemented by stacks of internal correspondence and case summaries tabled in the legislature.

They are now part of the official records of the Alberta legislative assembly, available for the public to read.

It is difficult to believe that these records are from leading hospitals in the capital city of a modern and fantastically wealthy province. The case descriptions, usually only a line or two, are attached to a series of emails from emergency-room physicians to top health-care executives and leading elected officials, including Alberta's minister of health and premier.

They cover the period from February to October 2008, and are deeply troubling to read:

"Fractured hip, severe pain, nowhere to off-load patient."

"No ICU beds in region, 3 admitted ICU patients in [emergency] department."

"Patient with chest pain, previous history of an MI [heart attack], had entire 8hr work-up and blood work in the waiting room. Never made it to a patient care area."

"7 EMS crews in waiting room for prolonged period of time with no movement…"

"88 year old female arrived with EMS at 1328, complaining of change in speech and CVA [stroke] like symptoms, no care area for assessment and treatment. During wait in waiting room with EMS awoke at 1710 with complete right side hemiparesis [paralysis] and an acute CVA [stroke]— out of the therapeutic window by hours when bed finally available."

"A patient presented with a VP shunt [a drain to relieve pressure on the brain] complication, and had to be placed in the waiting room for a prolonged wait. This patient was sitting in the waiting room with a VP shunt sticking out of her head."

"Riot at the Edmonton Max, had absolutely no reserve in the Emergency Department and we were receiving a number of unknown injuries from the riot, requested to activate the disaster plan and CH [Capital Health] executive on call refused."

These cases run for pages and pages of small print, yet they cover only a brief period at just two hospitals. Situations like these have been common in many Alberta hospitals for years.

A paralyzing misperception

For two decades, Alberta's health-care system has been kept in turmoil because of a misperception of out-of-control spending. This misperception means that, every so often, politicians and policy makers become frightened that health-care spending will grow to consume the entire provincial budget. They then send the system on a wasteful roller-coaster ride of cuts to staff, facilities and training. When these cuts inevitably create a crisis, the government launches a headline-grabbing surge in recruitment and construction.

Sometimes, politicians panic and do both at once, building shiny new hospitals while laying off large numbers of staff.

The government has displayed a similar pattern in managing its other responsibilities — education, for example. In June 2011, the Stelmach government announced $500 million in new school construction the same week that many hundreds of teachers lost their positions.

It would be comical if it weren't so serious.

This paralyzing push-pull dynamic has made government simultaneously more *expensive* than it should be — reinforcing the calls for cutbacks — and less *effective* than it should be — reinforcing the demands for more spending.

This has caused a shocking waste of money, time, talent, opportunity, progress, human well-being and even lives.

The chain that links government and citizens

If we really expect our politicians and our governments to make good decisions, to solve problems in the health-care system, to educate our children, and to manage our public wealth wisely, they need to have good information. A lot depends on it, including people's lives.

There are many links in the chain leading from misinformed politicians making wrong decisions based on bad information, to overcrowded hospital wards where people suffer unnecessarily and even die, but it is nonetheless surprisingly direct.

When you yank hard on one end of the chain, you hurt someone on the other end.

8

Education by the Numbers

ON JANUARY 19, 2010, THE *Calgary Herald* printed an article by Ken Boessenkool called "Join together with 'hands off my wallet.'"

In the article, Boessenkool says Albertans should call for cuts to public spending. He specifically targets education spending, making this remarkable claim: "We'd have to cut a whopping $4 billion to get our spending [on education] down to the level seen in Ontario."

This is an absurd statement. A $4 billion cut would eliminate forty percent of the funding for K-12 and post-secondary education in Alberta. Here's what a cut like that could look like. Post-secondary institutions in Alberta accounted for $3 billion in Alberta's 2011 budget. So, to save that $3 billion, we could start by pulling provincial funding from the University of Calgary — a total of $507 million, which would take out half its budget and eliminate a big chunk of matching funds as well. We would have to do the same to the University of Alberta, withdrawing $726 million — half its budget — plus matching funds. We would then have to gut SAIT, and then NAIT, and then every last one of the remaining twenty-two publicly funded colleges, technical schools and universities across the province. All of that would still fall a billion short, so we'd still have to lay off a few thousand teachers. And this, according to Boessenkool's numbers, would get us to the level of education spending that is normal in Ontario.[10]

Although these claims got published, they simply do not make sense. So, maybe there are other explanations for that $4 billion difference. For example, in Ontario, school taxes are handled locally, so they do not turn up on provincial accounts. On the other hand, in Alberta, school taxes flow up from local government through the provincial government, and then are redistributed back to school boards. So they do turn up on provincial accounts. This, of course, would make it look like provincial spending on education is far higher in Alberta than Ontario. But it would mostly be a matter of accounting.

Better evidence on education spending

What does the evidence on education spending really indicate? We ran the numbers to find out for ourselves.

Once provincial and local government spending on education is consolidated, Alberta's spending on education falls within a reasonable range compared to other provinces.

It's possible to subdivide education spending into a bunch of subcategories, but to keep things simple, we combined the spending from kindergarten right through to post-graduate. (We show K-12 and post-secondary separately in Table 7a and Table 7b at the back of this book.)

Graph 7 shows our results. Predictably, you see a drop in education spending in the mid-1990s. On this graph it looks small, but it was a real cut of 13 percent, which represents a lot of educators, facilities and programs. The cuts led to larger class sizes, deferred maintenance, and a virtual freeze on new construction for school boards and post-secondary institutions, even while Alberta's population was soaring. The cuts included slashing vocational programs at high schools, which may still be contributing to Alberta's high drop-out rates and shortage of trades workers. They also downsized medical and nursing faculties, which has had damaging long-term consequences for health-care delivery.

Even so, education didn't suffer the kind of drastic cuts seen in other sectors, such as health care. While the Klein government cut 13 percent

10 The 2011 budget of Alberta Advanced Education and Technology, and the 2010–11
    budgets of the University of Calgary and the University of Alberta, are all available online.

GRAPH 7. K-12 AND POST-SECONDARY EXPENDITURE PER CAPITA (2009$)

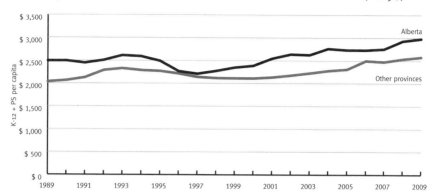

The Alberta government's per capita spending on education has been, overall, modestly higher than the Canadian average over the last twenty years. But a deeper look shows this is mostly due to our larger proportion of children.

from education from 1993 to 1996, it cut 25 percent from health care. (See Table 5 and Table 7 in the back of this book.)

More kids, more costs, more opportunities

Graph 7 appears to tell a slightly different story than some of the others we've looked at. In Alberta, spending on education consistently looks as if it has been above the average in other provinces.

But as with spending on health care, spending on education is heavily affected by the age of a population. Alberta has the youngest population in Canada, which bodes well for our future. But as a society, we pay up front. Those children need education: more school-age children mean more costs as well as more opportunities.

So, you would expect Alberta's younger population to drive up the costs of education. Sure enough — as an in-depth research paper from Statistics Canada shows — this is the case.

The research paper, published in 2010, analyzed "school indicators." It is loaded with statistics on schools and education by province. In some cases Alberta is high, in others it is low, but mostly it looks pretty much like the other provinces.

Among its reams of results, here are some highlights[11]:

- Alberta's spending per K-12 student was 3.1 percent higher than the Canadian average in 2008–09, and in the previous seven years had increased at a rate less than the Canadian average.
- Alberta was the only province that had an increase in its school age population from 2003 to 2009.
- Alberta's teachers are paid among the highest in the country when measured as straight salary.
- But Alberta has the most students per educator, so salaries per student are below the Canadian average.

When all is said and done, there is a lesson to this. Despite the noisy headlines and silly claims to the contrary, spending on education in Alberta isn't wildly out of line with the rest of the country. And it certainly doesn't reflect the enormous size of Alberta's economy.

---

11 The highlight facts come from "Summary Public School Indicators for Canada, the Provinces and Territories, 2002/2003 to 2008/2009" by Riley Brockington, Statistics Canada, 2010. The pages referenced are 23, 29, 30 and 41.

9

Tracking Public Money for
Housing and Social Services

Calgary, 2007. WE BOTH REMEMBER the incident well. It was a lovely

summer evening in Calgary in 2007, and my wife Jeanette Boman and

I were walking to a reception. Our hotel was in the Beltline just south

of downtown, and as we walked the few blocks north to our event, we went through the small railway underpass immediately west of the Palliser Hotel. We weren't in a rush, and with people passing us in both directions we didn't notice the man lying on the ground until we were right beside him.

He was stretched out awkwardly along the sidewalk's edge, wedged against the concrete wall of the underpass. We stopped, our formal evening wear a complete contrast to his torn and grubby garb. We bent to examine him carefully, and saw the slight rise and fall of his torso in the regular rhythms of sleep. So, taking our cue from the crowd, which had ignored him completely, we continued on.

The remarkable thing about that moment is how unremarkable it was. If you didn't look carefully, you could easily have taken the man for dead. But people didn't look — they just sidestepped and went on. It's not that they were callous. They were inundated.

At that time, people living and sleeping on the street were simply part of the daily streetscape of downtown Calgary, as people walked from their offices in Banker's Hall for lunch at the Petroleum Club, or shopped along Stephen Avenue. As I went about my business, I passed them every day. Most people felt as disturbed and helpless as I did, and public dismay grew steadily into calls for action.

It wasn't just a Calgary problem. In Edmonton, Jeanette and I once walked past a man lying at the edge of Jasper Avenue, as we went to a formal event in the Shaw Centre. When we left hours later, we realized he was comatose: he had not moved a muscle. We were with City Councillor Don Iveson and his wife Sarah Chan. Don called an ambulance and we waited until help arrived.

It's not just "street people" who are homeless. Working people and families are homeless, too. The forests around Ft. McMurray are sprinkled with the tents of working people who cannot afford a place to rent. Grande Prairie, Red Deer and smaller centres all have a problem that was unknown to them two decades ago: substantial numbers of people living without homes.

These anecdotes are reflected in the numbers. In Edmonton, from March 1999 to October 2008, the number of homeless people rose from 836 to 3,079. In Calgary, the number of homeless people soared from 447 in 1992 to 4,060 in 2008.[12]

None of this should be a surprise. That chain I've mentioned, the one that links the decisions of the government to the lives of its citizens, was pulled taut and then hauled hard in the middle 1990s, and it was pulled hardest for those who could least resist. No one felt the pain more than Alberta's most vulnerable people.

The evidence on housing expenditure

Housing represents a tiny portion of provincial expenditures, but it has a huge impact on people's lives. Graph 8 illustrates the CANSIM data on housing expenditures for Alberta, and for the rest of Canada. Look carefully and you will notice that, unlike the other graphs in this book, which measure spending by hundreds or thousands of dollars, spending on housing is measured in fifties. For governments, housing

---

12 Information about the numbers of homeless in Edmonton and Calgary in this section come from the following reports, available online: "Edmonton Biennial Homeless Count" and "City of Calgary 2008 Biennial Count of Homeless Persons."

GRAPH 8. HOUSING EXPENDITURE PER CAPITA (2009$)

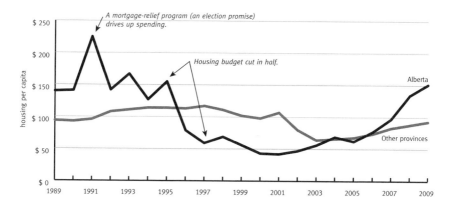

This graph compares government spending on housing in Alberta and in the rest of Canada. The Alberta government's spending on housing is a small part of its total spending. It has lurched above, and then far below, the Canadian average over the last twenty years. Meanwhile, thousands of people remain homeless in Alberta.

budgets are proportionately as small as pocket change. In the case of the Alberta government, it got to the point of picking the lint.

Graph 8 shows that spending on housing among the other provinces, adjusted for inflation, ranged from $94 to $117 per capita for all the 1990s. It then sagged as low as $64, no doubt in relation to cuts in federal housing supports, before recovering to $93 by 2009. (See Table 8 in the back of this book.)

Once again, the picture is volatile in Alberta — and discouraging. In a wild anomaly spawned by an election promise, Alberta's spending on housing spiked to more than double the national average in 1991. This paid for a program designed to subsidize mortgage rates that were roaring in the mid-teens. The target of this program wasn't the homeless or the poor, it was first-time homebuyers.

That blip lasted one year. Alberta's spending on housing then took a nosedive in the mid-1990s. In fact, between 1995 and 1996, the government slashed its housing spending almost precisely in half. In effect, Alberta's spending on housing all but disappeared for the ten years from 1996 to 2003. It bottomed out at $42 in 2001, and remained at $56 or lower every year from 1999 to 2003.

Each one of those numbers relates to a human story, a story that turns up in the face of a person living on the downtown streets or the river valley parks, of an anxious child crowded with her parents in a shelter, of a mentally ill person in an emergency room or jail cell.

In the spring and summer of 2007, tent cities appeared in the middle of Edmonton and Calgary. On August 11, 2007, the *Edmonton Journal* ran a headline declaring "Stelmach gov't flubbed housing crisis." The situation had become too embarrassing and the public outcry too loud. Municipal governments and non-profit groups launched new programs, and the Alberta government finally responded. Ed Stelmach, newly chosen as premier, appointed an all-party task force on affordable housing, and by 2008 Alberta's housing spending had risen markedly.

The crises in affordable housing and homelessness began to abate. From 2008 to 2010, for example, the homeless count in Edmonton fell from 3079 to 2421.

Things continue to get better, but we still have homeless people by the thousands, here in one of the richest places on earth.

The evidence on social-services expenditure

Shortly after getting elected, the Klein government took a knife to spending on social services. They did this by reducing benefit levels for rent and utilities. They lowered the standard allowance for food, clothing and transportation by $26 per month for each adult, as if poor people needing to eat were somehow the cause of the provincial debt, and making them hungrier would improve things. People drawing benefits were shown the door by the tens of thousands. The number of welfare clients plummeted from 94,087 to 34,959 between 1993 to 1997.[13]

Digging deeper into the data exposed one mystery we could not solve: in 1994–95, employee pension benefits dropped from a typical annual average of about $600, to zero. We didn't have the resources to track this further, but a spike the year before they disappear suggests there may have been some form of buyout. This accounts for the largest long-term portion of the cuts to social-services spending, and we do not have an explanation.

---

13 Peter Faid, *Poverty Reduction Policies and Programs; Extending the Alberta Advantage,* Canadian Council on Social Development, 2009.

GRAPH 9. SOCIAL-SERVICES EXPENDITURE PER CAPITA (2009$)

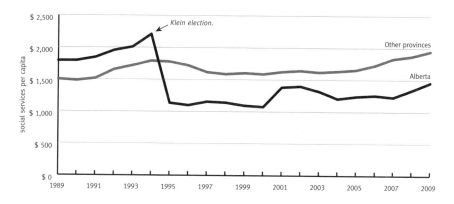

Spending on social services was cut dramatically by the Klein government, and has stayed consistently lower than the Canadian average ever since.

To thousands and thousands of Alberta's most vulnerable citizens, the cuts to social services, when combined with the cuts to housing, were a double whammy that hit hard, an abuse on top of many abuses already suffered.

10

It's Time for a Human Services Index

GOVERNMENTS ACROSS CANADA PLAN, fund and administer human services through many separate streams, which tends to fragment the ways we understand, plan and deliver human services. But the reality of human needs is not so tidy. Social problems overlap and reinforce one another.

Homeless people, for example, are often homeless because they struggle with mental illness. Children from impoverished households may do poorly in school because they are hungry. Seniors occupy beds in hospitals for months, if they have chronic illnesses and no place to live. Mentally ill people are discharged from emergency rooms because there are no beds available, only to wind up back in police custody, and eventually in courts and jails.

But government thinking, funding and programs typically treat these issues in isolation. Hospitals have little say on housing policies; police and courts struggle to find mental-health treatment for offenders; cuts are made to programs trying to pull children and families out of poverty, even though poverty correlates with poor health, higher crime, and lower educational achievement.

Alberta's government manages its human services through separate programs and completely different departments, as if the issues they engage are completely unrelated. Yet housing, health, education, justice, poverty, and social programs are profoundly interconnected.

Consider the amount the Alberta government spent per capita in 2009 on the following areas (2009$):

Health Care	$ 3,529
Education (K-PSE)	$ 3,217
Social Services	$ 1,456
Justice and Protection Services	$ 346
Housing	$ 151
Total	$ 8,698

An extra $38 a year would increase the budget for housing by a huge 25 percent, but would only add 1 percent to the health-care budget.

Where would those $38 have a bigger impact?

Who in government is asking questions like that?

Spending on human services not soaring

Let's bring together the five Statistics Canada categories of human services spending — health care, education, social services, housing, and justice and protection services — to create a single "human services index." Graph 10 shows what it would look like. Two things stand out.

- First, the increase in funding for human services in both Alberta and Canada has been very slow. For Alberta, the increase is from $6,820 in 1989 to $8,968 in 2009, or an average of 1.3 percent a year for the past twenty-one years.

- Second, from 1995 to 2009, funding in Alberta has stayed very close to the Canadian average.

Clearly, funding for human services is not soaring in Alberta, or in Canada. In Alberta, the rate of growth in human service spending falls far below the rate of economic growth.

A human services index like this encourages decision-makers to take a comprehensive approach to funding and programs that are focused directly on helping people live better — things like health, education, income supports, seniors, housing, police, courts, and other similar programs. And it helps cut through the myth that we somehow spend more on social programs than we can afford.

GRAPH 10. HUMAN SERVICES INDEX PER CAPITA (2009$)

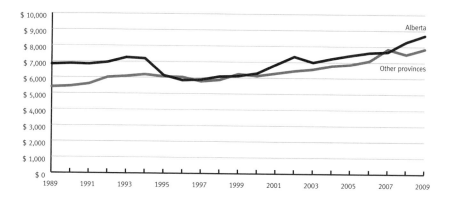

This graph shows how spending looks when you combine sectors such as health, education, social services and housing into one "human services index" — useful because spending in one sector of human services affects outcomes in other sectors. This index also confirms only a gradual climb in spending on human services.

11

Tracking Transportation and Other Spending

WHEN WE BEGAN RUNNING THE DATA in other areas, I was especially curious about Alberta's spending on roads. My regular driving routes had many construction zones, and the traffic talk on the radio gave constant updates on construction-related slowdowns. It seemed roads were getting repaired or built everywhere.

It made sense when I saw the numbers: from 2006 to 2009, spending shot up.

But as usual, Alberta's spending in this area has swung up and down dramatically, as Graph 11 shows. It fell 40 percent from 1989 to 1997, to a level where basic repairs to existing roads — let alone new-road construction — went neglected.

Then it jumped for three years, correlating with a rise in natural gas revenues and the 2001 election. This was followed by another collapse as the government overreacted to the 9/11 attacks. It cancelled so many projects that the road building industry had to sell off fleets of equipment and send workers packing. Then suddenly the party was back on. From 2005 to 2009, the Alberta government's spending in this area rose by more than 150 percent, rising from $408 per person to $1,029, far above the rest of the country.

GRAPH 11. TRANSPORTATION AND COMMUNICATION EXPENDITURE PER CAPITA (2009$)

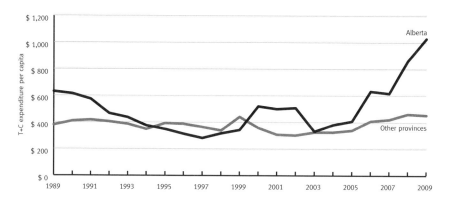

This graph shows the Alberta's government's spending on infrastructure such as highways, water pipelines, transit and telecommunications. In 2009, spending was well above the Canadian average. What stands out here, though, is how erratic the spending has been — at times so low that roads lacked basic repairs.

These swings almost certainly mean that Alberta taxpayers get worse value for their tax dollars, as road-building companies have quietly but firmly told me. Inadequate maintenance means that roads degenerate more than they should, driving up repair costs. Alberta Transportation's annual plans confirm that 42 percent of the province's highways are in fair to poor physical condition.[14] Short-term surges in spending add inflationary pressures, especially when they come on the heels of sudden cuts to the industry's capacity.

Despite the spending spikes, when the swings are averaged out, Alberta's spending on transportation and communication from 2000 to 2009 ranked fourth in the country. (See Table 11 in the back of this book.)

Other spending

As for other spending, we hunted through the data in three areas that StatsCan tracks. In two, Alberta's spending was higher than other provinces. You can see the details of this spending in Tables 11a, 11b and 11c in the back of this book.

---

14 In 2009–10, 58.1 percent of provincial highways were in good condition, 26.8 percent in fair condition, and 15.1 percent in poor condition. See *Government of Alberta Budget 2011 Strategic Plan and Ministry Business Plans*, page 114, available online.

One area of higher spending was the environment. It is consistently above average. This may be due to our resource-based economy, where most of our wealth is directly extracted from nature.

The second area of above-average spending is in what Statistics Canada calls "Resource Conservation and Industrial Development." This covers spending that supports economic development. From 1989 to 1993, Alberta's spending in this area was four to five times higher than the rest of the country, as billions of public dollars flowed to private businesses in everything from drilling subsidies to misguided investments in corporations like Gainers. Gainers received a $20 million loan from the government. When it defaulted, the government seized the Gainers plant and closed it.

The election of the Klein government shows here, too: by 1998, Alberta's spending in this area had dropped to near the Canadian average. Then it spiked in 2002 and 2003, when the government rescued the cattle industry from the BSE crisis. It has gradually declined since then, returning to levels similar to those in other provinces.

The third area we searched was spending on police, firefighting, courts, and corrections services. Despite any law-and-order image, the Alberta government has spent less than the average since 1991.

12

Tracking Money into Savings Funds

OUR HUNT THROUGH THE DATA HAD taken us a long way. One thing was clear, and frankly startling: only a small portion of Alberta's nation-leading economic growth of the past twenty years has gone to public services.

The heat of Alberta's economy had transformed the whole province — especially the long extraordinary surges in the Edmonton-Calgary corridor, the exploding growth of Grande Prairie, the hyper boom of Fort McMurray, and the sudden expansions of smaller centres from Hinton to Cold Lake. But all that economic growth had passed by Alberta's public services. In effect, Alberta was trying to run a 2009 government on a 1989 budget.

Recap: the evidence so far

The numbers sliced through the overblown claims of soaring public spending. Suddenly, much was explained: the congested hospitals, teacher layoffs, multiplying tuition fees, overcrowded courthouses, crumbling streets, and homeless people.

It's true that Alberta's spending had been at the top of the country throughout the 1980s and was more than average in 1989. But it's also true that Alberta's spending was below average for much of the following decade, and at times was at the bottom of the country. Getting up to the national average wasn't going to make up for our failure to invest in public programs during the 1990s.

Entire cities lived with this failure every day. For example, Grande Prairie, which is the referral centre for the Peace Region, was still coping in 2011 with a hospital built in 1986, while its population had grown from 27,000 to over 50,000. Fort McMurray's hospital was built in 1980, when 27,000 people lived there, too; in 2009, 89,000 lived there.

Calgary and Edmonton grew by hundreds of thousands of people each from 1989 to 2009, yet the number of hospital beds actually shrank. A similar point could be made for most other public services. Overcrowded emergency wards were just one symptom of a much larger problem.

Since 1993, the Alberta government has been living off the legacy of public facilities and services left over from the 1980s. That legacy has been worn to threads.

The Sustainability Fund and the Heritage Fund

Although Alberta's wealth had not gone to improving public services, there was still one place in the provincial government that it could have gone: savings. This was an important trail to follow, because we already knew the government had paid off its multi-billion-dollar debt.

I described the Alberta government's climb out of debt earlier, in Graph 2. The numbers behind that graph are impressive (see Table 2 in the back of this book). The net financial debt peaked in 1994, at $9.3 billion, and dropped to zero in 2000, when net debt turned to net savings.

Then, as annual surpluses kept piling up, the Alberta government began topping up some of its longstanding funds, including the Heritage Savings and Trust Fund, and created new funds and accounts. Savings flowed into funds that support research in areas like medicine and engineering, and that provide scholarships for students.

By 2008, the Alberta government's accumulated net financial position was $37 billion to the good.

Where is this money held? The consolidated financial statements of the Alberta government present a summary balance sheet, which provides a tidy list of the province's financial assets. In 2010–11, many of the government's financial assets were in accounts committed to specific purposes, including endowments and self-supporting financial organizations like the Agricultural Financial Services Corporation.[15]

When it comes to Alberta government savings, two funds are the real eye-catchers: the Alberta Sustainability Fund, and the Alberta Heritage Savings Trust Fund.

The Sustainability Fund held over $11 billion on March 31, 2011, but most Albertans don't know much, if anything, about it. They should. It has been the Alberta government's financial lifeline since 2008, rescuing the government from sinking into debt, raising taxes, or enacting much harsher austerity measures.

The Sustainability Fund was established in 2003 at the urging of then Opposition leader Ken Nicol, to cover off short-term drops in revenues. In fiscal emergencies, the government could dip into this fund rather than shut down services or borrow money. At first, it was capped at $2.5 billion, but as annual surpluses grew and grew, the cap was repeatedly raised.

The fund has worked as intended. The Stelmach government drew $5.6 billion out of it in 2009 and 2010, for example, to cover revenue shortfalls caused by low oil and natural gas prices and a slower economy. The Sustainability Fund's balance dropped from almost $17 billion to about $11 billion. The benefit: an injection of government funds to provide needed projects, services and jobs, without raising taxes or borrowing money.

Clearly, this fund is a great short-term stabilizer to offset Alberta's volatile economic swings. What about the long term?

THE HERITAGE FUND

The granddaddy of Alberta's savings funds is the Heritage Savings Trust Fund. It is the biggest, oldest and most famous. If the Sustainability Fund is a debit card for the Alberta government when there is an economic emergency, the Heritage Fund is, or at least could be, an RRSP that provides permanent prosperity. This is the fund that an impressive range of people and groups — including former premier Peter Lougheed, University of Calgary economist Jack Mintz, the Canada West Foundation, and the Alberta Liberal official Opposition — have said must grow very, very big, if Alberta's future is to be secured.

---

15 See the *Consolidated Financial Statements of the Government of Alberta, Annual Report 2010–2011*, available online.

So how is it doing?

Before we answer that question, let's set the scene.

THE EVIDENCE ON GOVERNMENT INCOME

Savings for governments are like savings for people: they are possible when income exceeds spending. We had reams of data on the spending half of this equation, but what about the income half? We had to go back to the CANSIM database and look at a new set of numbers on Alberta's revenues.

Look at Graph 12. The Alberta government's revenues per capita remained in a narrow range from the long period of 1989 to 2000. They spiked for one year, then dropped back to historic levels in 2002, from which they climbed substantially for several years.

In Alberta, the climb in government revenues from 2002 to 2008 is hardly surprising: the price of oil rose from US$19.69 a barrel in January 2002 to US$133.93 in June 2008. The price of natural gas during the same period rose from US$81.29 per thousand cubic meters to US$456.57. The result was a bonanza for the Alberta treasury, recorded in the government's consolidated financial statements: over $11 billion in non-renewable resource revenue in each of 2007 and 2008.

But, as fast as provincial government revenues grew, the economy grew even faster. So, as a portion of the GDP, government revenues were falling. Over the two decades, based on five-year averages, they dropped by about a fifth, from about 20 percent of GDP to about 16 percent. (See Table 12a in the back of this book.)

So, when measured as dollars per person, Alberta government revenues were up. When measured as a portion of the economy, they were down.

What had this meant for the fate of Heritage Savings Trust Fund? Up or down?

THE EVIDENCE ON GOVERNMENT SAVINGS

In March 2011, I was nominated by our Opposition caucus to serve on the Standing Committee on the Alberta Heritage Savings Trust Fund. This is one of the few all-party committees of the Alberta legislature, and although it is renowned for being one of the rubberiest of rubber-stamp committees, I was intrigued by the chance to get a closer look at a really important matter.

GRAPH 12. TOTAL GOVERNMENT REVENUE PER CAPITA (2009$)

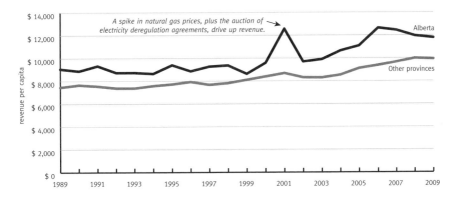

As this graph shows, Alberta's government has had consistently higher revenue than the rest of Canada over the last twenty years. This is thanks to its oil and gas resources. But compare this graph, which shows a slow climb in revenue, to Graph 1, which shows a steep climb in GDP (the total value of Alberta's economy). Why isn't Alberta's government, on behalf of Albertans, netting more revenue from Alberta's booming economy?

The Lougheed government first established the Heritage Fund in 1976, with the laudable goal of setting aside a portion of the royalties generated by non-renewable resources. The fund grew quite rapidly over the first decade, but slowed significantly after 1984, when the government reduced its contributions from 30 percent of royalties to 15 percent. It slowed even more three years later, in 1987, when natural resource revenue transfers stopped completely. Contributions to the fund resumed sporadically in 2006.

On my first day, I wanted to get a clear picture of the fund's performance over the course of its history. I had the fund's current value in front of me, as part of the latest report, but all those months with Mel and Junaid had reinforced the importance of adjusting for inflation and population.

I was a little concerned, as the new guy, about making enemies at my very first meeting. But I went ahead and asked, as gently as I could, if the ministry of Finance and Enterprise could provide the fund's value over its thirty-five-year history, adjusted for inflation and population.

I was grateful, and a bit surprised, when staff from the ministry replied, "We'd be happy to do that."

GRAPH 13. VALUE OF THE HERITAGE FUND PER CAPITA (2009$)

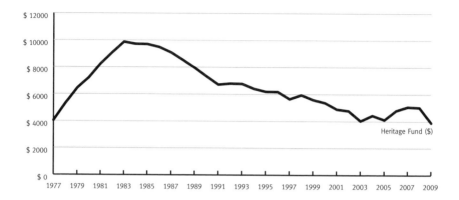

This graph shows that we can't track Alberta's wealth to the Heritage Fund. The Heritage Fund was established in 1976 as a reserve of funds for Alberta's post-petroleum future. Considering Alberta's booming economy, you'd expect — and hope, since our future prosperity depends on it — to see the line tracking up. Instead, measured per capita and adjusted for inflation, the fund is worth less today than when it was established.

So, Graph 13, above, comes not from CANSIM, but from the Alberta government's own records.[16] It shows the fair market value of the Heritage Fund's assets, per capita, inflation-adjusted by us to 2009 dollars.

For me, this is the most depressing information we produced: an almost unrelenting decline in the value of what is supposed to be this province's investment fund for the future.

The core story comes down to this: after adjusting for inflation, the Heritage Fund was worth more per Albertan in 1976–77, the year it was established, than it was in 2009–10. After 34 years, its value had dipped from $4,040 per person to $3,934 (2009$). Its peak was way back in 1982–83, when its value reached more than $9,870 per Albertan. It has been in decline ever since.

There are several reasons. The government reduced contributions to it and then eliminated them for many years. For more than half of the fund's existence, the government had made no provisions for inflation-proofing. The fund's earnings were pulled into general revenues rather

---

16 Memorandum to the Standing Committee on the Alberta Heritage Savings Trust Fund
    from Alberta Finance and Enterprise, June 16, 2011.

than staying to generate growth. And its management was uneven, reflecting its often confused mandate.

You could tell at a glance that Alberta's natural resource treasure wasn't going into the Heritage Fund. When it came to solving the mystery of where Alberta's wealth is going, one more door had been closed off.

Back on the money trail

Where was our investigation now?

First, measured as dollars per capita and adjusted for inflation, total spending on government programs is roughly the same as it was twenty years ago.

Second, government revenues have risen. This difference allowed the debt to be eliminated and substantial short-term savings to accrue into the Sustainability Fund, though very little went to the Heritage Fund.

Third, both spending and revenues have fallen as a portion of the GDP. By any measure, the Alberta government represents a smaller and smaller part of Alberta's economy.

We'd been following the money and the trail hadn't led to the public sector in any form — spending or savings. Where else could it lead?

13

Tracking Personal Incomes

WE HAD BEEN DIGGING THROUGH CANSIM data for two months, now.

Junaid had cranked out enough spreadsheets to make an accountant's

heart flutter. Mel's advice had kept us from following false leads down dead ends, which was a good thing, because I kept saying "What about this? What about that?" We squeezed time out of Christmas holidays and met on Saturday afternoons.

Connecting the lines on graphs to real-world events intrigued me. Junaid would send a graph with a sudden plunge in revenues, and I would realize it showed the dramatic short-term economic impact of the 9/11 attacks. Those attacks were in my first year as an MLA, and I remember debates within weeks of the attacks, about cutting crucial services and laying off people. It was graphic evidence that Alberta's economy, though strong, was brittle. It fed the Liberal official Opposition's commitment to promote the Sustainability Fund, which the government introduced two years later.

The graphs showed the government's substantial multi-year rise in spending to cope with the BSE crisis, and they showed the cost of political shenanigans. I smiled knowingly at the bumps in spending during election years.

We were writing a fiscal biography of the Alberta government, a government which had a character, and which responded in its own way as it went along, negotiating its course in a complicated world.

But we still hadn't figured out where Alberta's disproportionately large wealth was going.

Part of the answer

Where else could it be going? Right away I wondered about personal incomes. I often read reports on the juicy retail figures for Alberta, showing that we have more room in our wallets for everything from luxury cars to restaurant meals. It seemed reasonable to think that Alberta's wealth was flowing mostly to the bank accounts of people who live here.

What an idea! Alberta's wealth, going directly to us as individual citizens.

I had no idea how difficult this would be to find out. I'd worked with the CANSIM data from time to time for many years, but only on government spending and revenues. I didn't even know if it held data on personal incomes. It did, and Mel knew exactly where to send Junaid digging. Once again, we ran the Stats Canada numbers by province for the 1989 to 2009, adjusting for inflation and population.

In Graph 14, the top line shows average personal income. Over the last twenty-one years, average personal incomes in Alberta rose about 35 percent, even after accounting for inflation. That's pretty nice growth. It is not just a figment of my imagination — there really are more nice cars on the road, bigger houses in the suburbs, and more winter holidays to the tropics. Many Albertans are more prosperous than they were twenty years ago.

Averages can conceal a lot, though. If we just took the average temperature in Alberta winter would not exist, and if we just take the average income we would have no poverty. The real world does not work that way. I was reminded of the TD Bank study from 2005, which said that 42 percent of individuals living in Calgary had less than $20,000 a year. Inequality, as TD cautioned, is a real concern.

This twenty-one-year growth in average income contrasts with the stall in spending on public services we found earlier. Albertans live with

GRAPH 14. ALBERTA PERSONAL INCOME AND INCOME TAX PER CAPITA (2009$)

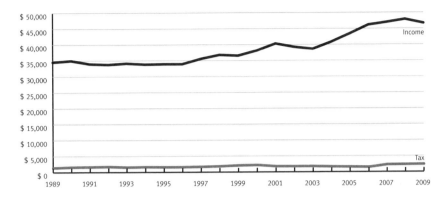

This graph shows that, on average, the personal incomes of Albertans have risen in the last twenty-one years. So, we can follow some of the money from Alberta's booming economy into Albertans' own pocket books. Not everyone has benefited from higher incomes, however. We know, for example, that 42 percent of individuals in Calgary lived on less than $20,000 a year in 2005.

this imbalance every day. We drive luxury cars on potholed streets, live in luxury houses but can't find a family doctor, return from Hawaii holidays to hold bake sales for the school library.

In Graph 14, the line at the bottom represents the provincial income tax paid by the mythical "average person." It illustrates how low, and how consistently low, provincial income taxes have been in Alberta, hovering around 5 percent of income. In the other provinces as a whole, provincial income tax averages 6 or 7 percent of income.

We were surprised at how low it was. I had to remind myself that it did not include federal taxes. When it comes to provincial income taxes, it would be hard to make the case that Albertans are overtaxed. You could even argue the opposite, that taxes are too low to sustain a modern government in the longer term. In other words, if we don't pay careful attention, there will be no avoiding a sizable tax jump in the future. We are spending Alberta's non-renewable resources to keep our taxes low today, and largely ignoring the risks of tomorrow.

Where's the rest?

At last we had found where some of Alberta's wealth was going. But, while incomes were up, they hadn't nearly kept pace with the growth of the economy. With the exception of the sharp slowdown in 2009, Alberta's economy had grown by about 70 percent per person in twenty years, even after adjusting for inflation. Our incomes only rose by 35 percent. So, even though we're individually more prosperous, a smaller and smaller portion of the economy went towards our personal incomes.

My mind, as it often does, turned its attention to pizza. I love food, and I love to use food metaphors. My wife and I raised two sons, and we learned early on to be fair when we divided up the food on pizza night. No matter how big the pizza was, we each got a fair portion.

So let's go back in time twenty years, and think of Alberta's economy as a medium pizza. Public services got two slices, personal incomes got two slices, and the rest of the pizza went elsewhere.

Today, we've gone from a medium to an extra-large pizza. But public services are still getting the same two slices. Our personal incomes are getting about three pieces, so we're doing a little bit better. But that leaves a huge amount of pizza left over.

The question still remained: who is eating the rest?

THE DOUBLE DAMAGE OF PUBLIC-SERVICE CUTS

Have you ever wondered what happened to the job of school nurse? Do you notice that the grass in parks doesn't get mowed until it seems ready for baling? Have you come to expect just the bare minimum from public services?

Our research offers an explanation.

Most public services by their nature are labour intensive. They are based on people: police officers, judges, teachers, professors, nurses, doctors, social workers, caregivers.

When the average personal income in Alberta grows by 35 percent in twenty years, while at the same time spending on public services grows by only 5 percent, there are just three options.

First, a government can refuse to increase wages in the public sector, so people working there will become poorer and poorer compared to everyone else. But it's an unlikely way to attract and keep an effective public service in the long term.

Or, second, a government can keep public-sector wage increases in line with everyone else's increases, but pay for fewer and fewer services and positions — for example, cut public housing, defer maintenance on roads, and eliminate school nurses and grass-cutting in parks.

Or, third, government can ask public servants to do more with less by improving productivity. Services can be automated, program duplications can be eliminated, and so on.

Any of these options can succeed a little bit, and at various times they might make sense. But none of them are without serious risks if carried too far.

Eventually, the habit of eroding public services becomes a path to broader decline.

If you think effective and professional public services are too expensive, picture the places in the world that don't have them. Would you rather live there?

14

The Answer Tracked Down

I WASN'T GOING TO GIVE UP. I returned to the TD Economics reports on Alberta's "tiger" economy. Both the 2005 and the 2007 versions calculated corporate profits as a share of Alberta's GDP. Profits had grown rapidly, the reports said. Page 2 of the 2005 report noted that corporate profits took "roughly twice the share [of GDP] posted in the rest of Canada." Maybe this was the clue.

Did CANSIM have the information? Could we do the same calculation for profits as we had for personal incomes? Mel said, "Sure," and Junaid went to work.

In a modern economy like ours, profitable corporations are generally good things. Profits finance economic growth, create jobs, and contribute taxes to help pay for public services. I'd rather have my money in a profitable bank than a losing one, and I'd rather depend on a job in a business that is in the black, than one in the red. When markets function properly, excessive profits soon flatten out as competitors move in for a piece of the action. That is how it is supposed to work, and how it usually does work.

In the heartland of capitalism — the United States — profits have consistently accounted for 8 to 12 percent of GDP since 1950. They sagged below that level for much of the 1980s and the early 1990s, when the U.S. was in the recession that pulled Alberta into debt. Only at the peaks of the richest booms have profits fleetingly moved a tiny bit above 12 percent of GDP.[17]

Holy smokes

I had a "holy smokes" moment when I opened Junaid's email with the data and graphs on profit trends. I double-checked that Junaid had sent me the right information. Corporate taxes and profits. Straight out of Statistics Canada. Adjusted for inflation and population growth. I emailed Mel to make sure I understood this information correctly.

Then I sat back in my office chair and took in the information on my computer screen. Is this really what happened? It looked like we had followed the money to the end of this particular trail.

I wish I had a way to animate that upper line, in slow motion. It shows the trend of profits in Alberta after correcting for inflation and population growth. Profits start in 1989 at $4,400 per capita. There was a little dip in the economy in the early 1990s. Then they climbed up to a little over $7,000 through the mid 1990s. Another little dip, and then a big spike in 2000 and 2001. By then, profits were more than 250 percent the level of 1989.

There's a drop after 2001, because of the after effects of 9/11. But profits quickly recovered and continued to rise. And, though the numbers weren't yet available at the time of writing, signs point to a similarly quick recovery after the downturn in 2008–09.

And so, by 2008, just before the downturn, profits in Alberta had gone up well over 300 percent, after adjusting for inflation and a larger population. This rate of increase was far faster than overall economic growth, which meant that profits increased from one-tenth of Alberta's GDP, to nearly a quarter.

This isn't corporate capital investment or total expenditures. This is profit. For every individual in Alberta, corporations were earning an average of $16,000 in profits per year from 2004 to 2008.

In fairness, that is profits before taxes, but it doesn't make much difference. The bottom line in Graph 15 is corporate income taxes per capita. It's very low, very flat.

---

17 J. Steven Landefeld and Shaunda Villones, "The Financial Crisis: It's all in the Official Statistics…Somewhere," Bureau of Economic Analysis, U.S. Department of Commerce, 2009, Figure 4.

GRAPH 15. ALBERTA CORPORATE INCOME AND INCOME TAX PER CAPITA (2009$)

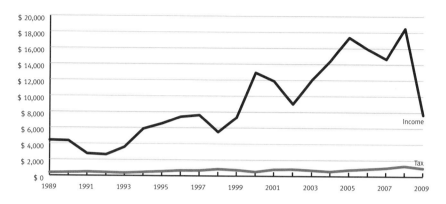

This graph shows that the income of corporations in Alberta has risen dramatically over the last twenty-one years. As Alberta's economy has boomed, so have profits — far more than government spending, government reserve funds for the future, or personal incomes. Corporate profits account for a bigger and bigger portion of Alberta's economic pie.

Corporate income taxes paid to the Alberta government rose modestly in absolute terms with the rise in corporate profits. But Alberta's corporate tax rates are low, and getting lower, so a smaller and smaller portion of profits went to the provincial government. In 2008, provincial income taxes represented about 7 percent of corporate profits — so, of the $66.5 billion in profits in 2008, corporations paid $4.7 billion in provincial income taxes.

And unlike personal income, or provincial government revenues and spending, corporate profits comprised a much larger portion of the GDP than twenty years before. In fact, they more than doubled their share of the economy from 1989 to 2008, rising from 9.6 percent to 22.8 percent.

At this remarkable level, the profits flowing to corporations are equivalent to the combined value of every single economic action in Alberta, beginning at one minute past midnight January 1, and ending on the morning of March 24. Every single economic activity includes transactions as small as buying a pack of gum, and as large as meeting the payrolls of the municipal, provincial and federal employees in Alberta.

In contrast, the taxes paid by corporations were a very small portion of GDP, and rose at a lower rate, from less than 1 percent of GDP to less than 2 percent of GDP.

Statistics Canada data indicate that, in 2008, profits per capita in Alberta were well over three times the average of $5,075 in the other nine provinces. (See Table 15a in the back of this book.)

While spending on public services in Alberta is very close to the Canadian average, profits in 2008 were 309 percent higher than the Canadian average, and have been far higher throughout the entire twenty years covered by the data.

To put this in a different way, in 1989, profits in Alberta were about equal to what the provincial government spent on health care. Twenty years later — in 2008, before the anomaly of the global financial crisis — they equalled everything the government spends, plus 70 percent more.

And Alberta's economy is so heavily defined by and dependent on petroleum wealth, it's clear these disproportionate profits come directly or indirectly from our publicly owned oil and gas resources.

This is no short-term blip driven by some surge in oil prices stemming from some Middle East conflict. This is structural, built into Alberta's economy over many years.

Profits are the return on capital, and there is no doubt Alberta has a capital-intensive economy. Those multi-billion-dollar oil sands plants represent some of the biggest capital projects in the world. In fact, Alberta has the most capital-intensive economy among all the provinces, 79 percent higher than the Canadian average.[18]

That may not be a surprise, but I think this is: Alberta ranks last in the country in terms of the productivity of that capital. From 1997 to 2007, Alberta's capital productivity fell from a disappointing 81 percent of the Canadian average to a dismal 61 percent.

So, Alberta's economy is tops in capital intensity, and yet dead last in the productivity of that capital. One possible explanation is that there is a time lag: the plants and projects driving Alberta's economy are still being built, so the capital is being spent now in order for the productivity to come later. But Alberta's capital intensity has been far

---

18 For figures on the capital intensity and capital productivity of Alberta's economy, see "Productivity and Competitiveness — Challenges for Canada and Alberta" by Andrew Sharpe, Centre for the Study of Living Standards. Sharpe presented this paper at the Imagining Alberta Symposium, Western Centre for Economic Research, University of Alberta, in October 2011. Available online.

above Canada's for a very long time. It was 43 percent higher than the Canadian level in 1997, for example. Any systemic time lag has presumably worked its way through.

Even more interesting, there has been no time lag in profits. They have been well above the Canadian average since as far back as our CANSIM data go.

Something is out of balance here, and some tough questions need to be asked.

If profits in Alberta are double the rates elsewhere in Canada and the United States, but capital is only 61 percent as productive, then where are those profits coming from?

If profits aren't coming from capital productivity, are they coming from the resource itself? Are the people of Alberta, who are the owners of the province's amazing petroleum wealth, leaving too much on the table, through either inadequate royalty or inadequate tax policies?

The Alberta government, knowingly or not, has arranged a series of policies that greatly favour one part of the economy over others.

Profits in Alberta have grown to rates simply unknown in other jurisdictions, often well beyond double the rates in other provinces and in the United States. There is no such largesse for public services, and the government is drawing down public savings rather than building them, doing nothing to prepare for the future.

This transfer of public wealth to private shareholders is blistering, and our own government, rather than fighting like an owner, or even thinking like an owner, is just happy to find investors who want to cash in.

CAN TOO MUCH PROFIT BE A PROBLEM?

There is a real risk that profit-to-GDP ratios in Alberta, when consistently double or more the rest of Canada and the United States, can distort economic decisions and warp the economy. This drives some serious economic questions to the surface.

- Where are these profits going? We looked for data that would answer that question, and we could not find it. For once, CANSIM let us down. It seems likely that a large portion leaves Alberta, and very possibly leaves Canada. To whose benefit?

- Do the extraordinarily high rates of profit generated by Alberta's economy encourage overinvestment here, overheating the economy, driving out other activities, and overloading infrastructure and other public services?

- Do these extraordinarily high rates of profit encourage investments that in normal situations would not be viable?

- Do the extraordinarily high rates of profit exacerbate Alberta's boom-and-bust cycle, and increase the risk of an investment bubble?

- If the government of Alberta has arranged a system that facilitates extraordinary corporate profits, why does it ask its citizens to settle for ordinary public services?

- Why doesn't the government save more?

These economic questions are serious, and need further investigation than we could possibly do in this project. There are still more fundamental issues, too. They concern justice and fairness, the nature of the society that Albertans want to create, and the need to have an honest debate if in the long run Alberta is to flourish.

15

Hard Truths

December 14, 1929, Ottawa and Edmonton. Canada's government agrees to give control of Alberta's land and resources to Alberta's government.

The fight had been hard. The issue of ownership of resources was crucial. Premiers and cabinet ministers, newspaper editors and mayors, lawyers, settlers, academics, clergy, and year-after-year the ordinary citizens of prairie Canada had debated and argued with each other, and even more with the federal government.

Alberta's premier John Brownlee and Canada's prime minister Mackenzie King finally hammered out the agreement in late 1929, in sometimes heated meetings. The final Memorandum of Agreement is unequivocal:

> In order that the Province [of Alberta] may be in the same
> position as the original provinces of Confederation...the
> interest of the Crown in all Crown lands, mines, minerals
> (precious and base) and royalties derived therefrom
> within the Province, and all sums due or payable for
> such lands, mines, minerals or royalties, shall...belong to
> the Province...

When this memorandum was passed into law as part of The Alberta Natural Resources Act, the climactic chapter in a long and hard-fought campaign was closed. The people of Alberta, through their government, owned outright their mineral resources. This was reinforced in the 1982 Constitution Act, which gave exclusive control of exploration, development, conservation and management of non-renewable natural resources to the legislatures of each province.

Owners, but not developers

So, for more than eighty years, the Alberta government has owned and controlled our oil and gas resources.

But, although it owns the resources, it relies entirely on others to develop them.

According to the Canadian Association of Petroleum Producers:

> A full 87 percent of the world's known oil reserves are state-owned or state-controlled — by countries like the members of OPEC and Russia.

> Only 13 percent (one barrel in six) is openly accessible to international oil companies. Almost half of that accessible oil — 6 of the 13 percentage points — is in Canada's oil sands.[19]

Maybe you noticed that CAPP's statement implies the oil sands are neither owned nor controlled by the government of Alberta. The oil sands are openly accessible to international oil companies, no doubt. But they are still owned and controlled by the people of Alberta through their government.

Presumably, CAPP's point is that Alberta contains almost half of the entire world's oil reserves that are available for free-market development. That makes our province a global hotspot for private-sector petroleum companies. If major private-sector oil companies want to grow their reserves and production, they likely head to Alberta.

Ironically, many state-owned or state-controlled corporations do likewise. These are corporations formed by other governments to fulfill national strategies. There is no guarantee they'll play by market rules if they don't want to. They are keen to make a good profit, but there can be other priorities too: supporting economic development back home,

19 David Collyer, president of the Canadian Association of Petroleum Producers (CAPP), gave these statistics in a presentation to the CAMPUT conference, May 2009. Available on CAPP's website.

securing energy supplies for their country, expanding global influence, and getting access to proprietary technology and expertise.

No matter for us, it seems — all comers welcomed. Although Alberta has no state-owned petroleum company of its own, it eagerly embraces billions of dollars in investments from many state-owned oil corporations from other places. For example:

- CNOOC (China)
- IPIC (Abu Dhabi)
- Korea National Oil Company (Korea)
- PetroChina (China)
- PTT (Thailand)
- Sinopec (China)
- Statoil (Norway)
- TAQA (Abu Dhabi)

The people of Alberta *did* once have a major state-owned petroleum company, Alberta Energy Company, and through the federal government they had part of another one, Petro-Canada. Though both companies were profitable, they were both privatized, regarded in some circles as unwise meddling in the market, as unfair competition for the private sector, and as socialist — or even communist. Petro-Canada's headquarters in Calgary was nicknamed "Red Square."

It's more than a twist, then, that we're happily letting other governments, including history's largest communist government, develop Alberta's oil and gas. Media reports in October 2011 indicated China had bought $28 billion worth of Canada's energy resources in the previous five years.[20]

It's not like Alberta's economy is short of capital to invest in resource development: on average, for the five years from 2004 to 2008, it generated corporate profits (*profits*, not revenues) at a pace of almost $1 billion every week. (See Table 15a at the back of this book.)

It's more like we Albertans and our government don't realize we own the resources under our feet. So, when outside developers get here, the Alberta government goes to great lengths to make them feel welcome. In fact, you might say, we bend over backwards.

---

20 See "Expert urges caution in Sinopec, Daylight energy deal," CBC News, October 11, 2011. Available online.

Giving it away

In October 2006, Murray Smith—acting as Alberta's official representative to the U.S. — was in Austin, Texas giving a speech and PowerPoint presentation to a room full of American energy experts. He mentioned that Alberta is the owner of its energy resources. He then summarized the government's approach to attracting development.

He said, "The model that has worked so well for us is that the royalty structure for oil sands is we 'give it away' at a 1 percent royalty structure and share in the risk of these great ventures and great investments. As soon as they reach payout, the royalty take goes to 25 percent of net..."[21]

In 2007, under growing public pressure, the government appointed a royalty review panel that included industry experts, who in turn hired international specialists in royalties and the energy industry. It's conclusion was clear: "...our review revealed that Albertan's do not receive their fair share from energy development and they have not, in fact, been receiving their fair share for quite some time."[22]

The report drew an angry reply from industry. After sharp and bitter debate in public and behind closed doors, the government tinkered with Alberta's royalty regime. Many changes were made, but the fundamental approach remained much the same — providing one of the most generous royalty and tax systems in the world.[23]

Nothing made this clearer than the change in the official goals of Alberta Energy, the government department that manages Alberta's oil and gas resources. Before the royalty review, there was a clear target published each year for royalty collection. For example, the department's 2007–10 business plan published a target of collecting 20 to 25 percent of the oil and gas industry's annual net operating revenue as royalty.[24] Every year, during question period and budget debates, I and my colleagues would rise in the legislature to challenge the government to meet their published goals, and every year the

---

21 From the transcription of a speech by Murray Smith, given at the annual meeting of the Interstate Oil and Gas Compact Commission (IOGCC) in Austin Texas, October 16, 2006.

22 *Our Fair Share*, Report of the Alberta Royalty Review Panel, September 18, 2007, page 4.

23 For further discussion, see for example "Alberta Department of Energy Business Plans, 2011–14," and the Report of the Auditor General of Alberta, April 2011, pages 35—39.

24 See "Budget 2007, Managing Our Growth," Government of Alberta, available online. Click "Government and Ministry Business Plans Index," and then "Energy." The royalty goals are on page 134.

government would fall short. It wasn't perfect, but these goals were a measure that allowed public accountability.

By the time the furore over the royalty review had died down, these goals were turned on their heads. It seemed the royalty system would no longer be measured by how it performed for the owners of the resource, the people of Alberta. Instead, it would be measured by how it performed for investors. For example, the department of energy business plan for 2011–14 has this goal for the royalty system: "Alberta will have a combined royalty and tax rate that is in the top quartile of investment opportunities compared to similar jurisdictions."[25]

As for the target of a 20 to 25 percent royalty on net operating revenues? Gone. Wiped from the books. In Alberta's new royalty system, there would be no target for how much royalty to collect on behalf of the owners — just a goal to make sure opportunities for investors were among the very best available.

So, we have created a very generous environment for petroleum corporations, both investor-owned and state-owned, an environment we nurture to this day — through subsidies, incentives and a resolutely favourable royalty structure. But to whose benefit? Are we thinking like owners? Or are we leaving too much on the table?

In 2010, the Canadian Association of Petroleum Producers forecast on its website that $1.07 trillion will be invested in Canada's oil and gas industry over the next twenty-five years. The association predicted this would drive $2.55 trillion of economic activity in Alberta. A trillion is a thousand billion.

---

25 See "Budget 2011, Building a Better Alberta," the Government of Alberta, available online. Click "Government and Ministry Business Plans Index," and then "Energy." The revised royalty goals are on page 54.

16

A Future to Build

Calgary, October 2004. I WAS AT A DINNER in Calgary. The restaurant had opened recently on the west edge of downtown, not far from the banks of the Bow River. I was a guest, and the easy banter among the six or eight business leaders I was meeting was fun to watch. The items on my menu had no price list, and the wine and conversation flowed in braided streams.

Everyone at the party depended one way or another on the energy sector for their business, and things were looking good. The global economy had recovered from the shock of the 9/11 attacks. The price of West Texas Intermediate crude oil, the benchmark price for Alberta, had just surpassed the dizzying level of US$50 a barrel. It felt historic, and spirits were high.

The link between the price of oil and the prosperity of the industry was captured in a pithy and tongue-in-cheek toast, when the man beside me raised his glass of wine to the group: "Here's to oil at $50 a barrel. It isn't just good for business, it makes us think we're smarter and better-looking, too."

As Alberta rides the crests and troughs of energy prices, more than its economy is at stake. As ironic and self-mocking as his comments were, my dinner companion knew that Alberta's identity, its very sense of self worth, had become tied to the price of oil and gas. That's a vulnerable place to be.

The fear and worry I saw across Alberta barely four short years later, when oil once again passed $50 a barrel, this time plunging down from over $130, was a warning.

More than personal fortunes and public budgets are at risk. For many Albertans, so is our sense of who we are. We no longer feel quite as smart or good looking.

And the reaction from some circles has been predictable: hastily bring in royalty and tax breaks, provide incentives, and if the government goes into debt, then lay off nurses and teachers and delay public-sector capital spending. The debates and passions have been heated.

It doesn't have to be this way.

What happened to the public interest?

We now had the answer to our question. Alberta's disproportionately large wealth wasn't going to public services or personal incomes, and it wasn't being saved for future prosperity, either. It was going to profits, and it was doing so at an astonishing rate.

To smooth out the ups and downs of individual years, let's take some five-year averages.

1989–1993 VERSUS 2005–2009

	1989–1993 Five-year average (per capita, 2009$)	2005–2009 Five-year average (per capita, 2009$)	Change (per capita, 2009$)	Change (%)
Health care	2,505	3,222	$717	28.6%
K-12 education	1,156	1,552	$36	2.4%
Post-secondary education	995	1,273	$278	27.9%
Heritage Fund	7,108	4,583	−2,525	−35%
Corporate profits	3,551	14,814	11,263	317.2%

This table looks at some key fiscal indicators in Alberta: the earliest five-year average (1989–1993), the most recent five-year average (2005–2009), and the percentage changes. All numbers are per capita in 2009 dollars.

Three things stand out here for me:

- Education for K-12 went up 2 percent. Two percent, total, in twenty years.

- Health care and post-secondary spending each rose about 28 percent in twenty years — a long-term average of 1.2 percent per year.
- And corporate profits went up 317 percent.

Follow the money long enough, and you will find where it's going.

Feeling betrayed

When I studied this information it was hard for me, as an Albertan, not to feel like my province was failing itself. I don't blame corporations — they're just doing their job. They would make profits like this everywhere if they could, but they are not allowed to.

I blame the trustee of the people's wealth, the government of Alberta, for failing its citizens, and their future.

It is worth repeating that the source of Alberta's wealth is its immense reserves of oil and gas, especially the oil sands. Per person, Alberta's reserves are far larger than even Saudi Arabia's.

It is also worth repeating that the people of Alberta own these resources through their government.

That's why people like former premier Peter Lougheed urge the provincial government to "think like an owner" when it comes to oil and gas development. We are the owners, dammit, and the stakes are too high to be this sloppy and weak.

Some people will celebrate the economic patterns we uncovered. They will argue that Alberta has prospered because it has pushed taxes down and squeezed public services. The more extreme voices will say it should go even further. They may twist the evidence until the facts themselves squeal shrill and hollow, about skyrocketing public spending and bone-crushing tax burdens. They may even carry the day, continuing to win the struggle to define political reality.

But the facts on the ground will not change. The real reason Alberta has prospered far beyond the rest of Canada and the rest of the developed world, is that it is home to some of the largest petroleum reserves in the world, at a time when the world is thirsty for petroleum.

Let's be honest. Alberta's situation cannot be sustained. Our society has become addicted to the wealth that flows from our petroleum. The government is addicted, the private sector is addicted, and we as individuals are addicted.

As with every addiction, this one will bring us down unless we confront it. We can either ease out of the habit with a clear goal, a good strategy, and tough-minded self-discipline. Or we can hang on, in denial, until the final bust.

A question we need to talk about

When Alberta's treasurer Lloyd Snelgrove delivered his budget speech to the legislative assembly on February 24, 2011, he made the usual boasts and promises, but for me and many others one quote stood out.

"With any other provincial tax system," Mr. Snelgrove claimed, "Albertans and Alberta businesses would pay at least $11 billion more in taxes each year…" In coming days and weeks I heard the government repeat this boast: the Alberta government's total tax take would rise by $11 billion if it were at the level of the next lowest province.

These are simplistic statements, but they illustrate a broad reality. The Alberta government could increase its taxes to collect many billions of dollars more per year, and still have the lowest taxes in Canada. And Canada in general, after years of corporate tax cuts, is a low tax jurisdiction for corporations.[26]

How low? In 2011, Alberta's total taxation on corporate income — federal and provincial taxes combined — was 26.5 percent of income, and Alberta's government projected it would drop to 25 percent in 2012. These numbers aren't even close to corporate income taxes in the United States, which is the biggest foreign market for Alberta's exports. In the U.S., federal and state corporate income taxes totalled 39.2 percent in 2011.[27]

Alberta's new premier, Alison Redford — elected as Tory leader in October 2011 — has promised to change the way the Conservatives govern Alberta. If she keeps her promise, the proof will be in the public policies that Redford's government backs — policies about Alberta's royalty regime, tax structure, plans to save for the future, and funding for public services.

Should the Alberta government raise taxes? Should it raise royalties on oil and gas? At the time of writing, the most recent quarterly

---

26 See, for example, Duanjie Chen and Jack Mintz, "Canada's 2010 Tax Competitiveness Ranking," University of Calgary School of Public Policy, February 2011.

27 See the report "Highlights of the Alberta Economy 2011," Alberta Finance and Enterprise, July 2011, page 30. Available online.

report from Syncrude's largest shareholder, Canadian Oil Sands Trust, reported that the company sold its crude for an average of $111 per barrel, and paid $10 per barrel in royalties.[28] That looks like a sweet deal for Syncrude (a significant portion now owned by the Chinese state), but what about for the people of Alberta?

How will the Alberta government close the gap between the way it lives today and the way it will be forced to live in the future?

In 2007, the Alberta government appointed the Financial Investment and Planning Advisory Commission. This commission submitted its report to the government in December 2007, and, in June 2008, followed it with a quiet but forceful letter to Iris Evans, who was then minister of finance. The letter, which was tabled in the legislature, points at a fiscal time bomb ticking beside Alberta's economic foundation. The crux of the letter is in this one sentence: "…the government today would need to hold net assets equal to $215 billion if it were to maintain existing public services and the Alberta tax advantage into the future."

In other words, if Alberta wants to permanently maintain its current public services without raising taxes or royalties, the Alberta government should have already banked $215 billion as a reserve. Given the immense economic activity in our province since the birth of the Heritage Fund — created in 1976 for exactly this reason, to create a reserve — that seems like an easily achievable goal. Yet, Alberta falls short of this target. Roughly $200 billion short.

Where will the government find that money?

It might be duped by the rhetoric of overspending on public services, and so lurch back into cutting health care, education and other services. Or it might not do anything, ignoring the warning signs until the crash landing can no longer be avoided.

Let's work toward something better.

Albertans face some unusually stark choices. We are on top of the world. We can stay the historic course and, like so many places throughout history, fall into painful and permanent decline. Or we can engage with the real issues, grasp the remarkable opportunities at our fingertips, confront the phantom threats, and build a future that goes from strength to strength.

Alberta's future is ours to build.

---

28 Canadian Oil Sands Limited Second Quarter Report, 2011.

Afterword: Dominion and Destiny

Fort Garry, Red River Colony, January 20, 1870. For the second day in a row, the crowd of a thousand people had assembled in the field enclosed by the palisades of Fort Garry, not far from the small settlement of Winnipeg. Nothing would deter them, neither the minus 20°F temperature, nor the aches from standing five hours on the trampled snow, listening as propositions for the future of western Canada were read aloud, in English and in French. This was their democracy, this was their provisional government, this was their land.

Dominating the platform were two men. Louis Riel, twenty-five years old, recently elected head of the newly declared Provisional Government; and Donald Smith, age forty-nine, Commissioner of the Hudson's Bay Company and delegate for the Government of Canada.

The previous year, the Government of Canada had bought the land that would form the bulk of western Canada from the Hudson's Bay Company. The people who lived on the land had not been consulted, and now they wanted a say. Under Riel's leadership, they had formed a provisional government and, with an armed patrol, had turned away at the border the first governor sent from Ottawa. So the federal government sent Smith as an emissary. He had thirty years experience in the fur trade, and a wealth of information from his local network. He was conciliatory, respectful and shrewd.

The provisional government had prepared a list of rights as a condition of accepting the rule of Canada. High on the list: transferring control and ownership of crown land, including mineral rights, from the federal government to the proposed Province of Manitoba.

Smith, a fur trader married[29] to the daughter of a fur trader, carried the day, reassuring the assembled citizens that he would take their concerns to Ottawa, as indeed he did. He was sympathetic enough that, on his return to Ottawa, the hardliners in the government of John A. MacDonald regarded his mission as a disappointment. It would be 60 years before the prairie provinces got ownership and control of crown land. In contrast, Donald Smith, his Hudson's Bay Company, and soon the Canadian Pacific Railway, would do very much better.

Two men, different destinies

The lives of Riel and Smith were entwined that winter, but their startlingly different destinies speak to tensions at the core of this country. Riel was elected three times to parliament to represent Manitoba, but never took his seat in Ottawa, for fear of being arrested or murdered in Ontario for his role in the Red River Resistance. Instead, for almost a decade, he lived a life of exile in the United States, mired in poverty, taking odd jobs to support his family, and struggling with his health.

Riel returned to the Canadian west in 1884 at the invitation of the Metis living in Batoche, Northwest Territories (now Saskatchewan). They had never forgotten his leadership during the Red River Resistance, and many of the same issues were boiling again, this time further west. A year later, these tensions broke into violence in the Northwest Rebellion. The rebellion was defeated in May 1885, at the battle of Batoche. Riel turned himself over to the Canadian militia, and he was tried before judge and jury later that year. The jury found him guilty, and the judge passed what would become the most contentious sentence in Canadian history: "…you be taken to the place appointed for your execution, and there be hanged by the neck till you are dead." Louis Riel was hanged in Regina on November 16, 1885. He was forty-one years old.

Fortune was kinder to Donald Smith. Just nine days before Riel was executed, he drove the ceremonial last spike in the mountains of British Columbia to complete the Canadian Pacific Railway. He had become a

---

29 Smith and his wife, Isabella Hardisty, did not marry "legally" until they were grandparents in their seventies. She died in 1913.

leader in the CPR through his investments in railways during the 1870s, first in the U.S. and then in Canada. In 1887, he became president of the Bank of Montreal, a major financial supporter of the CPR, and held the post until 1905.

Smith had started at the bottom of the Hudson's Bay Company in 1838, age eighteen, and worked his way to the top the hard way, spending more than twenty years with the company's operations in Labrador. In the 1860s he was promoted to Montreal, and by the 1880s he was the company's largest shareholder, then served as its governor from 1889 to his death in 1914.

Like Riel, Smith was elected to parliament; unlike Riel, he felt confident enough to actually take his seat. But eventually he abandoned electoral politics to pursue business.

Smith's business interests were strategic. He was drawn to railways because they made it feasible to settle the prairies, and for Donald Smith that was vital. Through a complicated arrangement, the Hudson's Bay Company was granted 4.5 million acres of western land by the Government of Canada as part of the government's purchase of the company. The CPR was granted a staggering 25 million acres to help it finance railway construction. In both cases the grants included mineral rights.

The mineral rights meant that Smith's happy convergence of railways, banking, and land development eventually grew into mining, and then, when gas was discovered in 1891 near Medicine Hat, oil and gas. He rose to international status, served as Canada's High Commissioner in London, and raised a regiment from western Canada — Lord Strathcona's Horse — to serve in the Boer War in 1900–01. In 1909, at age eighty-eight, Smith became Chairman of the Anglo-Persian Oil Company, the forerunner of British Petroleum and the first company to strike oil in commercial quantities in the Middle East.

Smith died of heart failure in 1914, at the age of ninety-three. He had become one of the wealthiest, most powerful, and respected men in the English-speaking world.

Power, property, and petroleum

And what did destiny hold for the land that Riel and Smith had contested on that wintry platform in January 1870? Whose dominion would hold sway?

The Hudson's Bay Company was granted 4.5 million acres in 1869; the CPR was granted 25 million acres in 1880. The grants included mineral rights, and allowed the companies to slowly and strategically select the specific land they wanted. The CPR didn't make its final selection of land until 1903, when it claimed a block of three million acres east of Calgary. A decade later most of the surface lands had been sold and settled; the "Last Best West" was filled with farms, villages and small cities. But beneath the ground, a lot was still at play.

In 1926, the Hudson's Bay Company set up a separate company to manage the oil and gas resources acquired through its land grants. In 1982, Hudson's Bay Oil and Gas was sold to Dome Petroleum. Dome, in turn, was sold to Amoco in 1988, for $5.5 billion. In 1998, Amoco merged with British Petroleum in what was then the largest industrial merger in world history.

It was the closing of a grand cosmic circle, for BP is the direct descendant of the Anglo-Persian Oil Company; the corporate offspring of the land grants to Donald Smith's Hudson's Bay Company had merged with the direct corporate descendant of the Anglo-Persian Oil Company he chaired some ninety years before. BP's website speaks of their extensive natural gas operations in western Canada, which is built on the valuable heritage of the Hudson's Bay land grants. They are also a growing player in the oil sands.

For its part, the CPR spun off its oil and gas properties into a separate company in 1958. This eventually operated under the name Pan-Canadian Petroleum, and in 2002 this company merged with Alberta Energy Company to form Encana. Through the CPR land grants, Encana owns the mineral rights to millions of acres in southern Alberta, in regions originally served by the CPR. The holdings are so widespread that the Freehold Owners Association claims on its website that "it is virtually impossible for an oil company of any significant size to operate in southern Alberta without dealing with Encana."

Encana's other parent, Alberta Energy Company, was itself the beneficiary of massive public sector support when it was established in 1973 by then premier Peter Lougheed. This included a $250 million injection of capital from the Alberta government; 1000 square miles of natural gas–rich land in the Suffield area; a stake in Syncrude (at the time a high-risk venture); and an assurance from then energy minister Don Getty that the Treasury Branches, in effect a government-owned bank, "will enthusiastically cooperate with the government in making this company a success."[30]

In 2009, Encana split off its huge natural gas properties into a new company called Cenovus.

There is, then, a direct line from the massive land grants of the Hudson's Bay Company and the CPR, to some of the giants of Canada's energy sector. The business foundations of the tower built in Calgary as the headquarters for Encana and Cenovus rest at their deepest on public policy decisions made in Ottawa in the 1860s and 1880s, and in Edmonton in the 1970s, to transfer massive public wealth into private ownership.

As for the rest of the prairie land, that which lay outside the direct ownership of Hudson's Bay Company and the CPR, a struggle arose. If the people were going to own this land through their provincial governments, they were going to have to fight for it — 1870 was only the start.

Fighting like owners

There is an abiding bond in Canada between the democratic vitality of governments, and the active public ownership and control of lands and resources. Long before Confederation, when control of colonial governments began to gradually pass from appointed governors responsible to London, to elected assemblies responsible to the local citizens in the colonies of Nova Scotia, New Brunswick, and Upper and Lower Canada, two related principles were established: first, that self-governing colonies should administer their lands and resources, and second, that the benefits of doing so should belong to that colony.

The original provinces of Confederation had these rights and benefits confirmed when Canada was formed in 1867, and British Columbia was automatically granted them when it joined Canada in 1871.

But when the prairie provinces asked for the same, they were denied. The federal government's refusal came down to this: the prairies were too sparsely populated, at least with settlers of European descent; the threat of takeover from the United States was too great; the need to grant vast tracts of land to railways to pay for their construction was too compelling; and the control of immigration and settlement policy

---

30 Alberta Hansard, December 7, 1973, starting page 78. Getty's speech notes that the other owners of mineral rights in the Suffield block are none other than Canadian Pacific Railway and the Hudson's Bay Company.

was too crucial to the future of the entire country, to turn it over to the relatively small number of prairie settlers.

From 1869 to 1930, this issue of control over land and resources outraged western Canadians. It added fuel to the Red River Resistance and the Northwest Rebellion; rippled through every provincial and federal election on the prairies from 1870 to 1930; stoked regional resentments against Ottawa; and upon its success, laid the foundation for Alberta's rocketing rise to prosperity and power.

The debates raged across the entire country. Every province waded in, and both Liberals and Conservatives shifted policies as political fortunes and issues ebbed and flowed.

By 1930, the prairies were blanketed with farms, the population had soared, the railways were built, and the United States had been held at bay. The rationale for the federal position had dissolved.

The prairie provinces finally carried the day. They got ownership and control of their land and resources, including oil, natural gas and the oil sands.

And because of this transfer of resources, as the years went by, the government of Alberta got rich.

Richer than either it, or its citizens, seems to understand.

REFERENCES FOR AFTERWORD

An Act respecting the Transfer of the Natural Resources of Alberta. 1930. Legislative assembly of Alberta, Edmonton, Alberta.

Brownlee, John E. "The Transfer of Alberta's Natural Resources." Interview conducted by Una MacLean Evans, Alberta History, Autumn, 2005. Glenbow Archives, Calgary, Alberta.

Edmonds, Everard W. "The Natural Resources Question: A Plea for the Completion of Alberta's Status as a Province of Canada." Pamphlet. 1922. Henry Roche Printing Company Ltd., Edmonton, Alberta.

Flanagan, Thomas, and Mark Milke. "Alberta's Real Constitution: The Natural Resources Transfer Agreement." Pages 165–189, in *Forging Alberta's Constitutional Framework*. Richard Connors and John M. Law, eds. 2005. University of Alberta Press.

Foster, Peter. *Other People's Money.* 1983. Collins, Toronto.

Howard, Joseph Kinsey. *Strange Empire.* 1952/1994. Minnesota Historical Society Press, St. Paul, Minnesota.

Lyon, Jim. *The Rise and Fall of the House that Jack Built.* 1983. Macmillan of Canada, Toronto.

Martin, Chester. *The Natural Resources Question, The Historical Basis of Provincial Claims.* 1920. The King's Printer, Province of Manitoba.

McDonald, Donna. *Lord Strathcona : a biography of Donald Alexander Smith.* 1996. Dundurn Press. Toronto.

Report of the Royal Commission on the Natural Resources of Alberta. March 12, 1935, Ottawa, Canada. Hon. A.K. Dysart, Chairman.

Facts Found on the Money Trail

Percentage of world's known oil reserves open to development from private or outside corporations: **13**%

Percentage of those oil reserves in Alberta's oil sands: **46**%

Number of petroleum corporations owned by Alberta developing Alberta's oil sands: **0**

Publicly or state-owned corporations from other jurisdictions developing Alberta's oil sands: **at least 8**

Rank of Alberta and Saudi Arabia as owners of the world's known, developed oil reserves: **2, 1**

World ranking of Alberta's economy and Luxembourg's economy in 2008, measured as GDP per capita: **2, 1**

Growth in Alberta's economy from 1989–93 to 2005–09, measured as GDP per capita and adjusted for inflation: **67**%

Change in public spending in Alberta between 1989–93 and 2005–09 as a portion of GDP, adjusted for inflation: **-39**%

Public spending per capita in Alberta as five-year averages for 1989–93 and 2005–09 (2009$): **$10,119, $10,209**

Change in average personal incomes in Alberta from 1989 to 2009, adjusted for inflation: **+35**%

Percentage of individuals in Calgary living on less than $20,000 a year in 2005: **42%**

Change in the number of homeless people in Calgary from 1992 to 2008: **+800%**

Public spending per capita on social-services programs in Alberta in 1989 and 2008 (2009$): **$1,792, $1,338**

Rank of Alberta among Canada's ten provinces in health-care spending in 2010, measured per capita: **3**

Rank of Alberta among Canada's ten provinces in health-care spending in 2010, measured as a percentage of GDP: **10**

World rank of Canada for portion of GDP spent on private health care in 2010: **5**

World rank of Canada for public spending on health care in 2010: **18**

Fort McMurray's population in 1980, when its current and only hospital was built: **27, 000**

Change in Fort McMurray's population from 1980 to 2009: **+229%**

Per-capita value of the Heritage Fund in 1989 and 2009 (2009$): **$7,598, $3,900**

Corporate profits in Alberta as a percentage of GDP in 2007: **22.8%**

Corporate profits in the rest of Canada as a percentage of GDP in 2007: **12.2%**

Corporate profits in the U.S., as a percentage of GDP, since 1950: **8% to 12%**

Growth in corporate profits in Alberta from 1989 to 2008, before the global financial crisis, adjusted for inflation: **+319%**

Amount by which corporate profits in Alberta exceeded the total spending of the Alberta government in 2008: **70%**

Rank of Alberta in terms of taxation rates among Canada's ten provinces in 2010, from highest to lowest: **10**

Approximate additional annual taxes Alberta could collect and still have the lowest provincial taxation rates in Canada (2011$): **$11 billion**

Data Tables and Supplementary Information

The tables in this section present the data used to generate the charts in the book, as well as supplemental information of interest.

The tables are numbered to correlate with the graphs in the book. So, Table 1 provides the data for Graph 1, and so on.

Supplemental tables and graphs also have correlated numbering: Table 2a provides data related to Table 2 and Graph 2, for example.

A WORD ABOUT TABLE TERMINOLOGY

CPI stands for Consumer Price Index. The CPI is a tool for tracking inflation and is used to adjust the dollar values in the tables to 2009 dollars.

Real means that numbers are adjusted for inflation, which allows you to compare data from different years.

Nominal means that numbers are unadjusted for inflation

Per capita means "per person," and is calculated based on population data.

CA means "all the provinces in Canada." It *does not* refer to Canada's federal government.

Others means "all provinces in Canada except Alberta."

DATA FOR CALCULATING REAL AND PER-CAPITA VALUES

The CPI and population data used to calculate real and per-capita values are the same for every table. So, to simplify things, we have presented these data here — once.

CA CPI 2009=100	AB CPI 2009=100	CA pop	AB pop	CA – AB pop
65.4	58.4	27,276,781	2,498,325	24,778,456
68.5	61.7	27,691,138	2,547,788	25,143,350
72.4	65.3	28,037,420	2,592,306	25,445,114
73.4	66.3	28,371,264	2,632,672	25,738,592
74.8	67.0	28,684,764	2,667,292	26,017,472
74.9	68.0	29,000,663	2,700,606	26,300,057
76.6	69.5	29,302,311	2,734,519	26,567,792
77.7	71.1	29,610,218	2,775,133	26,835,085
79.0	72.5	29,905,948	2,829,848	27,076,100
79.8	73.4	30,155,173	2,899,066	27,256,107
81.2	75.2	30,401,286	2,952,692	27,448,594
83.4	77.8	30,685,730	3,004,198	27,681,532
85.5	79.6	31,019,020	3,058,017	27,961,003
87.4	82.3	31,353,656	3,128,364	28,225,292
89.9	85.9	31,639,670	3,183,396	28,456,274
91.5	87.2	31,940,676	3,239,471	28,701,205
93.5	89.0	32,245,209	3,322,200	28,923,009
95.4	92.4	32,576,074	3,421,253	29,154,821
97.5	97.0	32,929,733	3,512,691	29,417,042
99.7	100.1	33,315,976	3,591,391	29,724,585
100.0	100.0	33,720,184	3,670,742	30,049,442

Table 1

TABLE 1. PROVINCIAL GDP PER CAPITA: ALBERTA AND THE OTHER
PROVINCES (2009$)

Year	CA GDP (000,000 $)	AB GDP (000,000 $)	CA – AB GDP (000,000 $)	Others real GDP per capita ($)	AB real GDP per capita ($)
1989	657,728	67,377	590,351	36,438	46,216
1990	679,921	73,257	606,664	35,207	46,580
1991	685,367	72,892	612,475	33,257	43,028
1992	700,480	74,936	625,544	33,099	42,908
1993	727,184	81,179	646,005	33,184	45,428
1994	770,873	88,041	682,832	34,658	47,953
1995	810,426	92,036	718,390	35,312	48,395
1996	836,864	98,634	738,230	35,401	49,981
1997	882,733	107,048	775,685	36,254	52,169
1998	914,973	107,439	807,534	37,124	50,480
1999	982,441	117,080	865,361	38,823	52,710
2000	1,076,577	144,789	931,788	40,365	61,966
2001	1,108,048	151,274	956,774	40,026	62,155
2002	1,152,905	150,594	1,002,311	40,625	58,488
2003	1,213,175	170,113	1,043,062	40,791	62,190
2004	1,290,906	189,743	1,101,163	41,921	67,200
2005	1,373,845	219,810	1,154,035	42,660	74,366
2006	1,450,405	238,886	1,211,519	43,573	75,544
2007	1,529,589	255,787	1,273,802	44,428	75,041
2008	1,599,608	291,577	1,308,031	44,121	81,121
2009	1,527,258	247,184	1,280,074	42,599	67,339

The numbers in this table show the statistics used to calculate the
figures in the final two columns: per capita GDP in the rest of Canada
and per capita GDP in Alberta.

Even in the late 1980s and early 1990s, when the gap was at its
narrowest, Alberta's economy generated roughly $10,000 a year more,
per capita, than the average of the rest of Canada.

From that point on we see the gap widen. By the time we hit the
2008–09 economic downturn, Alberta's per-capita GDP was nearly
double that in the rest of Canada. Even after the downturn, Alberta's
economy generated an extra $25,000 per person in 2009 — more than
one and a half times the national average.

For decades, our provincial economy has been generating the kind of wealth other provinces couldn't possibly dream of. Why don't we see that reflected in our hospitals, our schools, our roads — or in our society in general?

Table 2

TABLE 2. PROVINCIAL GOVERNMENT DEBT PER CAPITA: ALBERTA AND THE OTHER PROVINCES (2009$)

Year	CA debt (000,000 $)	AB debt (000,000 $)	CA – AB debt (000,000 $)	Others real debt per capita	AB real debt per capita
1989	101,510	1,221	100,289	6,190	838
1990	112,015	3,512	108,503	6,297	2,233
1991	116,652	2,342	114,310	6,207	1,382
1992	143,065	4,152	138,913	7,350	2,377
1993	173,691	7,646	166,045	8,529	4,279
1994	202,446	9,346	193,100	9,801	5,091
1995	224,041	8,513	215,528	10,594	4,476
1996	235,896	7,084	228,812	10,972	3,590
1997	241,746	4,022	237,724	11,111	1,960
1998	245,223	1,603	243,620	11,200	753
1999	258,271	391	257,880	11,569	176
2000	256,157	-2,504	258,661	11,205	-1,072
2001	241,813	-9,983	251,796	10,534	-4,102
2002	249,431	-9,118	258,549	10,479	-3,541
2003	255,888	-10,575	266,463	10,421	-3,866
2004	259,988	-14,345	274,333	10,444	-5,081
2005	259,014	-19,661	278,675	10,301	-6,652
2006	252,534	-27,643	280,177	10,077	-8,742
2007	242,183	-34,974	277,157	9,667	-10,260
2008	241,364	-36,694	278,058	9,379	- 10,209

CANSIM provided data on provincial debt up to 2008, which is why this table has no data for 2009.

By the year 2000, the Alberta government had paid down enough debt and built up enough savings to become a net creditor. This process began in 1994 when Alberta's debt peaked at $5,091 per capita. From then on, Alberta steadily and aggressively reduced its debt, and eventually began building up net savings. By 2008 — the most up-to-date year available for this Statistics Canada data — the Alberta government had net savings of $10,209 per capita, or a total of almost $37 billion.

Alberta's performance here is far better than the average of the other provinces. In 2008, the average debt for the other provinces, $9,379 per capita, was almost the same as Alberta's net surplus.

TABLE 2A. PROVINCIAL GOVERNMENT ANNUAL SURPLUSES AND DEFICITS PER CAPITA: ALBERTA AND THE OTHER PROVINCES (2009$)

Year	CA (000,000 $)	AB (000,000 $)	CA – AB (000,000 $)	Others real per capita ($)	AB real per capita ($)
1989	-4,242	-1,486	-2,756	-170	-1,019
1990	-3,083	-1,981	-1,102	-64	-1,260
1991	-7,636	-1,078	-6,558	-356	-636
1992	-22,317	-2,123	-20,194	-1,069	-1,216
1993	-24,540	-3,127	-21,413	-1,100	-1,750
1994	-22,339	-2,467	-19,872	-1,009	-1,344
1995	-15,341	983	-16,324	-802	517
1996	-10,276	1,255	-11,531	-553	636
1997	-6,688	2,654	-9,342	-437	1,293
1998	-3,260	2,912	-6,172	-284	1,368
1999	-10,339	1,203	-11,542	-518	542
2000	2,134	2,683	-549	-24	1,148
2001	12,485	7,667	4,818	202	3,150
2002	-8,682	-832	-7,850	-318	-323
2003	-10,131	2,634	-12,765	-499	963
2004	-7,337	4,393	-11,730	-447	1,556
2005	7,467	5,262	2,205	82	1,780
2006	8,030	8,820	-790	-28	2,789
2007	9,364	9,117	247	9	2,675
2008	7,951	4,684	3,267	110	1,303
2009	-8,602	1,195	-9,797	-326	326

The 1993 decision by the Klein government to eliminate provincial government deficits shows clearly in Table 2a. In 1993, the Alberta government ran a deficit of $1,750 per capita, continuing a series of deficits that had begun several years before. A short two years later, the provincial government ran a surplus of $517 per capita.

Alberta is dangerously vulnerable to international forces. A striking example of this is the sudden deficit of $323 per capita in 2001–02. A single event — the 9/11 attacks — sent a shudder through the global economy. The annual price of oil fell twenty percent, from $30 a barrel to $24. More importantly for Alberta, the annual price of natural gas fell by a third, from $5.76/GJ to $3.74/GJ.

Table 3

TABLE 3. TOTAL PROVINCIAL GOVERNMENT EXPENDITURE PER CAPITA: ALBERTA AND THE OTHER PROVINCES (2009$)

Year	CA expenditure (000,000 $)	AB expenditure (000,000 $)	CA – AB expenditure (000,000 $)	Others real expenditure per capita ($)	AB real expenditure per capita ($)
1989	138,346	14,687	123,659	7,633	10,074
1990	148,971	15,933	133,038	7,721	10,131
1991	162,418	16,868	145,550	7,903	9,957
1992	177,115	17,375	159,740	8,452	9,949
1993	183,752	18,731	165,021	8,477	10,482
1994	187,551	18,337	169,214	8,589	9,988
1995	190,266	16,884	173,382	8,523	8,878
1996	193,090	16,230	176,860	8,481	8,224
1997	189,953	16,364	173,589	8,113	7,975
1998	193,197	17,016	176,181	8,099	7,995
1999	210,136	17,957	192,179	8,622	8,084
2000	213,952	19,704	194,248	8,415	8,433
2001	225,645	22,933	202,712	8,480	9,423
2002	238,505	25,785	212,720	8,622	10,014
2003	249,176	24,452	224,724	8,788	8,939
2004	261,398	25,683	235,715	8,974	9,096
2005	271,525	27,511	244,014	9,020	9,307
2006	292,477	31,150	261,327	9,399	9,851
2007	310,033	33,313	276,720	9,651	9,773
2008	331,019	38,294	292,725	9,874	10,654
2009	350,184	42,058	308,126	10,254	11,458

The data in this table do not show that Alberta's government spending has soared. They show no clear trend except erratic swings.

It is possible to juggle the figures to claim both that spending has dropped in the long term, or to show that it has jumped.

Average spending for 2005–09 was $10,208 per capita, while the average for 1989–93 was $10,119. In other words, despite impressions and rhetoric, Alberta's government spent almost the same per person in recent years as it did two decades ago.

Table 4

Table 3 shows that Alberta's spending per capita was essentially the same in 2009 as it was in 1989, once we adjust for inflation. In contrast, Alberta's economy grew dramatically, far faster than population growth and inflation. In other words, while Alberta's economy soared, per capita provincial spending flatlined.

This means that over the past two decades, government spending became smaller and smaller as a portion of the economy. This is shown in Table 4. As a society, Alberta spent a steadily shrinking portion of its increasing wealth on provincial public services.

For the five years from 1989–93, Alberta government spending averaged 22.6 percent of GDP. For the five years 2005–09, it averaged 13.7 percent of GDP. This is a 39 percent downsizing of the provincial government as a portion of Alberta's economy.

Here are the numbers on spending from other provinces over the last twenty years, for comparison:

- Ontario's spending has ranged between about 16 and 21 percent of GDP.
- B.C.'s has ranged between about 19 and 24 percent.
- Manitoba's has ranged between about 24 and 30 percent.
- Saskatchewan's spending shows a long-term decline even more dramatic than Alberta's. It dropped from a high of almost 35 percent of GDP in 1992, to below 17 percent in 2008, reflecting the resource boom in that province.

TABLE 4. TOTAL PROVINCIAL GOVERNMENT EXPENDITURE AS A PERCENTAGE OF GDP: ALBERTA AND THE OTHER PROVINCES (2009$)

Year	CA GDP (000 000 $)	AB GDP (000 000 $)	CA expenditure (000,000 $)	AB expenditure (000 000 $)	CA – AB GDP (000,000 $)	CA – AB expenditure (000,000 $)	Others expenditure/ GDP (%)	Alberta expenditure/ GDP (%)
1989	657,728	67,377	138,346	14,687	590,351	123,659	20.95%	21.80%
1990	679,921	73,257	148,971	15,933	606,664	133,038	21.93%	21.75%
1991	685,367	72,892	162,418	16,868	612,475	145,550	23.76%	23.14%
1992	700,480	74,936	177,115	17,375	625,544	159,740	25.54%	23.19%
1993	727,184	81,179	183,752	18,731	646,005	165,021	25.54%	23.07%
1994	770,873	88,041	187,551	18,337	682,832	169,214	24.78%	20.83%
1995	810,426	92,036	190,266	16,884	718,390	173,382	24.13%	18.34%
1996	836,864	98,634	193,090	16,230	738,230	176,860	23.96%	16.45%
1997	882,733	107,048	189,953	16,364	775,685	173,589	22.38%	15.29%
1998	914,973	107,439	193,197	17,016	807,534	176,181	21.82%	15.84%
1999	982,441	117,080	210,136	17,957	865,361	192,179	22.21%	15.34%
2000	1,076,577	144,789	213,952	19,704	931,788	194,248	20.85%	13.61%
2001	1,108,048	151,274	225,645	22,933	956,774	202,712	21.19%	15.16%
2002	1,152,905	150,594	238,505	25,785	1,002,311	212,720	21.22%	17.12%
2003	1,213,175	170,113	249,176	24,452	1,043,062	224,724	21.54%	14.37%
2004	1,290,906	189,743	261,398	25,683	1,101,163	235,715	21.41%	13.54%
2005	1,373,845	219,810	271,525	27,511	1,154,035	244,014	21.14%	12.52%
2006	1,450,405	238,886	292,477	31,150	1,211,519	261,327	21.57%	13.04%
2007	1,529,589	255,787	310,033	33,313	1,273,802	276,720	21.72%	13.02%
2008	1,599,608	291,577	331,019	38,294	1,308,031	292,725	22.38%	13.13%
2009	1,527,258	247,184	350,184	42,058	1,280,074	308,126	24.07%	17.01%

Table 5

TABLE 5. PROVINCIAL GOVERNMENT HEALTH-CARE EXPENDITURE PER CAPITA: ALBERTA AND THE OTHER PROVINCES (2009$)

Year	CA health expenditure (000,000 $)	AB health expenditure (000,000 $)	CA – AB health expenditure (000,000 $)	Others real health expenditure per capita ($)	AB real health expenditure per capita ($)
1989	36,557	3,551	33,006	2,037	2,436
1990	40,237	3,867	36,370	2,111	2,459
1991	43,854	4,119	39,735	2,158	2,431
1992	48,154	4,386	43,768	2,316	2,511
1993	49,963	4,800	45,163	2,320	2,686
1994	50,588	4,543	46,045	2,337	2,474
1995	50,793	4,179	46,614	2,291	2,197
1996	52,185	3,989	48,196	2,311	2,021
1997	52,386	4,245	48,141	2,250	2,069
1998	55,491	4,708	50,783	2,335	2,212
1999	59,607	5,154	54,453	2,443	2,320
2000	62,834	5,741	57,093	2,473	2,457
2001	67,947	6,148	61,799	2,585	2,526
2002	73,669	7,186	66,483	2,695	2,791
2003	79,229	7,664	71,565	2,799	2,802
2004	84,973	8,422	76,551	2,914	2,983
2005	89,556	8,896	80,660	2,982	3,010
2006	94,323	9,825	84,498	3,039	3,107
2007	102,031	10,673	91,358	3,186	3,131
2008	108,241	11,987	96,254	3,247	3,335
2009	115,501	12,954	102,547	3,413	3,529

Over the period covered by this table, Alberta spent, on average, $2,642 per capita each year on health care. The average for the other provinces over that period was very similar — $2,583. Once again, Alberta falls squarely in the mid-range for provincial spending.

Of course, Alberta's average spending tells only part of the story. From 1995 to 2001, our province slashed per capita health-care spending to levels well below the national average. Then, for the following five years, it pumped money back into the system, which brought Alberta back up to par. Erratic spending patterns like these translate into needless (and costly) turmoil in the health care system.

TABLE 5A. 2008 AGE-ADJUSTED PROVINCIAL GOVERNMENT HEALTH-CARE EXPENDITURE PER CAPITA, FROM CIHI (2009$)

Province	2008 per-capita spending ($)
Alberta	4,205
Newfoundland	3,886
Manitoba	3,635
Saskatchewan	3,565
Ontario	3,354
Nova Scotia	3,337
New Brunswick	3,313
B.C.	3,252
P.E.I.	3,109
Quebec	2,943

This table presents 2008 data, the most up-to-date available from the Canadian Institute for Health Information (CIHI).

Spending on health care is affected by the age of a province's population. In general, the higher the proportion of elderly people in a population, the greater the need for spending on health care.

CIHI adjusts provincial spending on health care to reflect the different age structures of each province. Because Alberta has a younger population than other provinces, but spends nearly the same per capita as other provinces, it effectively spends more on health care, vying with Newfoundland and Labrador for top spot.

CIHI's age-adjusted calculations for Alberta's health spending are higher in comparison to the unadjusted figures from Statistics Canada.

TABLE 5B. SPENDING ON SPECIFIC GOVERNMENT HEALTH-CARE
COMPONENTS PER CAPITA: ALBERTA (2009$)

Year	AB real health expenditures per capita			
	Hospital care ($)	Medical care ($)	Preventive care ($)	Other health services ($)
1989	1,241	981	36	178
1990	1,214	1,008	39	197
1991	1,037	1,079	39	276
1992	1,072	1,121	40	278
1993	1,206	1,153	40	287
1994	1,027	1,137	34	277
1995	852	1,037	39	269
1996	773	897	50	300
1997	872	873	48	276
1998	732	860	103	515
1999	802	833	78	606
2000	752	866	82	757
2001	758	906	89	773
2002	847	1,035	100	809
2003	874	1,068	96	763
2004	1,052	1,093	101	737
2005	1,137	1,142	117	614
2006	1,061	1,160	119	768
2007	1,139	1,159	111	723
2008	1,209	1,176	118	832
2009	1,262	1,184	130	953

Statistics Canada divides public-health spending into four major
components, in order to reveal the underlying trends in total health-care
spending. We included this table because it presents deeper patterns
in Alberta's spending, plus a big and growing piece of spending that
needs more explanation.

- Alberta's spending on *hospital care* has followed a roller-coaster
  path for the past twenty years, as the government spent and
  cut, spent and cut. From $1,241 per person in 1989, it fell to
  $1,037 two years later, then rose to $1,206 in 1993, only to be
  sliced to $773 in 1996. After a one-year rise of 13 percent it fell
  to its lowest modern level, $732 per capita in 1998. **That is a
  41 percent drop in spending per capita on hospital care over
  ten years.**

- Spending on *hospitals* then rose modestly in 1999, then fell back to near-record lows in 2000 and 2001. Since then, it has risen sporadically, rising quickly to $1,137 per capita in 2005, then dropping slightly, then rising again to $1,262 by 2009. After all the ups and downs, the Alberta government spent almost exactly the same per capita on hospitals in 2009 as it did in 1989 — but in the interim, spending was generally much lower.

- Public spending on *medical care* — such as physician treatment and public drug programs — also swung significantly up and down, moving within a range of $800 to $1,200 per capita. It has not varied as erratically as spending on hospital care, but it is difficult to see a clear long-term trend.

- *Preventive care* takes a consistently very small portion of health spending. While it rose in the past twenty years, 2009's record high was still a paltry $130 per capita.

- The most marked rise in Alberta's health-care spending has been in the category of *other health services*. Having stayed consistently below $300 per person each year from 1989 to 1997, it began to rise sharply in 1998. By the year 2002, spending in this area had shot up to $809. Since then, its rise has slowed: by 2008 it reached $832.

This category is the only category to show a large sustained cost increase in the past twenty years, and accounts for easily the largest part of the long-term increase in Alberta's health care spending.

What does this category include? Among many things it includes lab services, administration, ambulances, expenditures on ancillary enterprises, and grants to health-oriented organizations. Given the data available for this research, it is not possible to know which specific areas have been driving up costs, or why, but it is an important area for further analysis.

Clearly, though, the answers to rising health-care spending need not lie in sacrificing hospital care, medical care or preventive care.

Table 6

The portion of its GDP a jurisdiction spends on health care is recognized around the world as a useful measure of health-care spending. As this table shows, Alberta spends a smaller portion of its GDP on publicly funded health care — often a *much* smaller portion — than the average for Canada's other provinces.

TABLE 6. PROVINCIAL GOVERNMENT HEALTH-CARE EXPENDITURE AS PERCENTAGE OF GDP: ALBERTA AND THE OTHER PROVINCES (2009$)

Year	CA GDP (000,000 $)	AB GDP (000,000 $)	CA health expenditure (000,000 $)	AB health expenditures (000,000 $)	CA – AB GDP (000,000 $)	CA – AB health expenditure (000,000 $)	Others health expenditure/GDP (%)	AB health expenditure/GDP (%)
1989	657,728	67,377	36,557	3,551	590,351	33,006	5.59%	5.27%
1990	679,921	73,257	40,237	3,867	606,664	36,370	6.00%	5.28%
1991	685,367	72,892	43,854	4,119	612,475	39,735	6.49%	5.65%
1992	700,480	74,936	48,154	4,386	625,544	43,768	7.00%	5.85%
1993	727,184	81,179	49,963	4,800	646,005	45,163	6.99%	5.91%
1994	770,873	88,041	50,588	4,543	682,832	46,045	6.74%	5.16%
1995	810,426	92,036	50,793	4,179	718,390	46,614	6.49%	4.54%
1996	836,864	98,634	52,185	3,989	738,230	48,196	6.53%	4.04%
1997	882,733	107,048	52,386	4,245	775,685	48,141	6.21%	3.97%
1998	914,973	107,439	55,491	4,708	807,534	50,783	6.29%	4.38%
1999	982,441	117,080	59,607	5,154	865,361	54,453	6.29%	4.40%
2000	1,076,577	144,789	62,834	5,741	931,788	57,093	6.13%	3.97%
2001	1,108,048	151,274	67,947	6,148	956,774	61,799	6.46%	4.06%
2002	1,152,905	150,594	73,669	7,186	1,002,311	66,483	6.63%	4.77%
2003	1,213,175	170,113	79,229	7,664	1,043,062	71,565	6.86%	4.51%
2004	1,290,906	189,743	84,973	8,422	1,101,163	76,551	6.95%	4.44%
2005	1,373,845	219,810	89,556	8,896	1,154,035	80,660	6.99%	4.05%
2006	1,450,405	238,886	94,323	9,825	1,211,519	84,498	6.97%	4.11%
2007	1,529,589	255,787	102,031	10,673	1,273,802	91,358	7.17%	4.17%
2008	1,599,608	291,577	108,241	11,987	1,308,031	96,254	7.36%	4.11%
2009	1,527,258	247,184	115,501	12,954	1,280,074	102,547	8.01%	5.24%

Table 7

TABLE 7. K-12 AND POST-SECONDARY EXPENDITURE PER CAPITA: ALBERTA AND THE OTHER PROVINCES (2009$)

Year	CA expenditure (000,000 $)	AB expenditure (000,000 $)	CA – AB expenditure (000,000 $)	Others real per capita ($)	AB real per capita ($)
1989	36,605	3,632	32,973	2,035	2,491
1990	39,502	3,923	35,579	2,065	2,494
1991	43,340	4,146	39,194	2,128	2,447
1992	47,635	4,382	43,253	2,289	2,509
1993	50,017	4,670	45,347	2,329	2,613
1994	49,836	4,758	45,078	2,288	2,592
1995	50,954	4,742	46,212	2,272	2,493
1996	50,689	4,476	46,213	2,216	2,268
1997	50,371	4,539	45,832	2,142	2,212
1998	50,937	4,839	46,098	2,119	2,274
1999	52,327	5,217	47,110	2,114	2,349
2000	54,331	5,579	48,752	2,112	2,388
2001	57,233	6,195	51,038	2,135	2,545
2002	60,512	6,792	53,720	2,177	2,638
2003	64,112	7,180	56,932	2,226	2,625
2004	67,669	7,799	59,870	2,279	2,762
2005	70,601	8,077	62,524	2,311	2,733
2006	78,068	8,635	69,433	2,497	2,731
2007	80,342	9,386	70,956	2,475	2,754
2008	85,747	10,530	75,217	2,537	2,930
2009	88,426	10,940	77,486	2,579	2,980

Alberta's overall spending in education (K-12 and post-secondary) has been relatively stable, avoiding the sharp drops and surges in other areas of spending.

This table and the following table combine provincial and local spending on K-12 education, to compensate for the wide range of funding models across the provinces.

TABLE 7A. PROVINCIAL GOVERNMENT EXPENDITURE ON K-12 EDUCATION PER CAPITA: ALBERTA AND THE OTHER PROVINCES (2009$)

Year	CA expenditure (000,000 $)	AB expenditure (000,000 $)	CA – AB expenditure (000,000 $)	Others real per capita ($)	AB real per capita ($)
1989	23,567	2,106	21,461	1,325	1,445
1990	25,326	2,301	23,025	1,336	1,463
1991	27,898	2,512	25,386	1,378	1,483
1992	30,908	2,711	28,197	1,492	1,552
1993	32,603	2,928	29,675	1,524	1,639
1994	32,177	3,014	29,163	1,480	1,642
1995	33,195	3,058	30,137	1,481	1,608
1996	32,694	2,772	29,922	1,435	1,405
1997	32,690	2,798	29,892	1,397	1,364
1998	32,732	2,931	29,801	1,370	1,377
1999	33,030	3,207	29,823	1,338	1,444
2000	33,700	3,347	30,353	1,315	1,432
2001	35,134	3,571	31,563	1,320	1,467
2002	36,435	3,965	32,470	1,316	1,540
2003	37,972	4,247	33,725	1,319	1,553
2004	39,447	4,473	34,974	1,331	1,584
2005	40,659	4,538	36,121	1,335	1,535
2006	46,421	4,882	41,539	1,494	1,544
2007	46,828	5,318	41,510	1,448	1,560
2008	49,083	5,488	43,595	1,470	1,527
2009	50,195	5,855	44,340	1,476	1,595

Alberta's spending on K-12 education dipped from the early 1990s to the mid 1990s, and then modestly climbed from a low in 1997 of $1,377 per capita, to $1,595 in 2009.

TABLE 7B. PROVINCIAL GOVERNMENT EXPENDITURE ON POST-SECONDARY EDUCATION PER CAPITA: ALBERTA AND THE OTHER PROVINCES (2009$)

Year	CA expenditure (000,000 $)	AB expenditure (000,000 $)	CA – AB expenditure (000,000 $)	Others real per capita ($)	AB real per capita ($)
1989	13,038	1,526	11,512	711	1,047
1990	14,176	1,622	12,554	729	1,031
1991	15,442	1,634	13,808	750	965
1992	16,727	1,671	15,056	797	957
1993	17,414	1,742	15,672	805	975
1994	17,659	1,744	15,915	808	950
1995	17,759	1,684	16,075	790	885
1996	17,995	1,704	16,291	781	863
1997	17,681	1,741	15,940	745	848
1998	18,205	1,908	16,297	749	896
1999	19,297	2,010	17,287	776	905
2000	20,631	2,232	18,399	797	955
2001	22,099	2,624	19,475	815	1,078
2002	24,077	2,827	21,250	861	1,098
2003	26,140	2,933	23,207	908	1,072
2004	28,222	3,326	24,896	948	1,178
2005	29,942	3,539	26,403	976	1,197
2006	31,647	3,753	27,894	1,003	1,187
2007	33,514	4,068	29,446	1,027	1,193
2008	36,664	5,042	31,622	1,067	1,403
2009	38,231	5,085	33,146	1,103	1,385

Alberta's real per capita spending on post-secondary education fell 19 percent from 1989 to 1997, from $1,047 to $848. It then commenced a steady climb, reaching $1,403 per capita in 2008, before dipping slightly in 2009.

Table 8

TABLE 8. PROVINCIAL GOVERNMENT EXPENDITURE ON HOUSING PER CAPITA: ALBERTA AND THE OTHER PROVINCES (2009$)

Year	CA expenditure (000,000 $)	AB expenditure (000,000 $)	CA – AB expenditure (000,000 $)	Others real per capita ($)	AB real per capita ($)
1989	1,732	204	1,528	94	140
1990	1,816	221	1,595	93	141
1991	2,141	382	1,759	96	225
1992	2,284	248	2,036	108	142
1993	2,462	298	2,164	111	167
1994	2,481	234	2,247	114	127
1995	2,618	294	2,324	114	155
1996	2,518	155	2,363	113	79
1997	2,632	122	2,510	117	59
1998	2,559	146	2,413	111	69
1999	2,391	124	2,267	102	56
2000	2,366	101	2,265	98	43
2001	2,662	102	2,560	107	42
2002	2,085	121	1,964	80	47
2003	1,790	152	1,638	64	56
2004	1,941	195	1,746	66	69
2005	2,037	184	1,853	68	62
2006	2,312	242	2,070	74	77
2007	2,700	330	2,370	83	97
2008	3,102	480	2,622	88	134
2009	3,345	553	2,792	93	151

In Alberta, spending on housing consumes a very small portion of the provincial budget. From a high of $225 per capita in 1991, spending on housing seemed almost in danger of disappearing for the ten years from 1996 to 2006, reaching a low of $42 in 2001, and staying below $60 every year from 1999 to 2003. In 2007 and 2008, in the midst of a housing crisis, spending rose to $97 and $134 respectively, still below the level of every year from 1989 to 1993. 2009 saw another increase.

When compared to other provinces, Alberta's spending on housing is below average. From 2000 to 2009, Alberta spent an average of $78 per capita. The average for the other provinces was $82, and Saskatchewan spent the most at $167.

Table 9

TABLE 9. PROVINCIAL GOVERNMENT EXPENDITURE ON SOCIAL SERVICES PER CAPITA: ALBERTA AND THE OTHER PROVINCES (2009$)

Year	CA social-services expenditure (000,000 $)	AB social-services expenditure (000,000 $)	CA – AB social-services expenditure (000,000 $)	Others real social-services per capita ($)	AB real social-services per capita ($)
1989	26,913	2,612	24,301	1,500	1,792
1990	28,356	2,822	25,534	1,482	1,794
1991	31,033	3,125	27,908	1,515	1,845
1992	34,664	3,414	31,250	1,654	1,955
1993	37,008	3,590	33,418	1,717	2,009
1994	39,362	4,056	35,306	1,792	2,209
1995	38,348	2,157	36,191	1,779	1,134
1996	38,020	2,166	35,854	1,719	1,098
1997	36,912	2,367	34,545	1,615	1,154
1998	36,920	2,428	34,492	1,586	1,141
1999	38,152	2,429	35,723	1,603	1,094
2000	39,115	2,512	36,603	1,586	1,075
2001	42,168	3,361	38,807	1,623	1,381
2002	44,094	3,599	40,495	1,641	1,398
2003	44,952	3,605	41,347	1,617	1,318
2004	46,300	3,399	42,901	1,633	1,204
2005	48,432	3,666	44,766	1,655	1,240
2006	51,980	3,971	48,009	1,727	1,256
2007	56,705	4,189	52,516	1,832	1,229
2008	60,316	4,808	55,508	1,872	1,338
2009	63,843	5,344	58,499	1,947	1,456

The numbers in this table show the depths of the cuts to social-services spending under the Klein government. In 1994, the government cut spending in half, which put it well below the Canadian average — and where it remains today.

Table 10

We have broken the data for Graph 10 into two tables, one for Alberta and one for the other provinces. To compare the human services index for Alberta with the Canadian average, focus on the last column in each table.

Alberta's five-year averages for 1989–93 and 2005–09 show an increase from $6,947 to $8,000 — about 15 percent. This seems more than affordable, considering the growth in Alberta's economy over the last twenty-one years.

TABLE 10. HUMAN SERVICES INDEX PER CAPITA: ALBERTA (2009$)

Year	AB health expenditure per capita ($)	AB social-services expenditure per capita ($)	AB education expenditure per capita ($)	AB protection of persons and property expenditure per capita ($)	AB housing expenditure per capita ($)	Index ($)
1989	2,436	1,792	2,141	311	140	6,820
1990	2,459	1,794	2,127	346	141	6,866
1991	2,431	1,845	2,044	292	225	6,837
1992	2,511	1,955	2,035	310	142	6,954
1993	2,686	2,009	2,093	304	167	7,259
1994	2,474	2,209	2,104	276	127	7,191
1995	2,197	1,134	2,425	228	155	6,139
1996	2,021	1,098	2,393	240	79	5,830
1997	2,069	1,154	2,332	264	59	5,878
1998	2,212	1,141	2,401	258	69	6,080
1999	2,320	1,094	2,400	245	56	6,114
2000	2,457	1,075	2,477	237	43	6,289
2001	2,526	1,381	2,646	234	42	6,829
2002	2,791	1,398	2,860	256	47	7,351
2003	2,802	1,318	2,588	227	56	6,990
2004	2,983	1,204	2,738	238	69	7,231
2005	3,010	1,240	2,841	279	62	7,433
2006	3,107	1,256	2,859	313	77	7,612
2007	3,131	1,229	2,918	291	97	7,666
2008	3,335	1,338	3,178	309	134	8,294
2009	3,529	1,456	3,217	346	151	8,698

Table 10 continued on next page…

TABLE 10 (*continued*). HUMAN SERVICES INDEX PER CAPITA: THE OTHER PROVINCES (2009$)

Year	Others health expenditure per capita ($)	Others social-services expenditure per capita ($)	Others education expenditure per capita ($)	Others protection of persons and property expenditure per capita ($)	Others housing expenditure per capita ($)	Index ($)
1989	2,037	1,500	1,489	268	94	5,389
1990	2,111	1,482	1,481	277	93	5,443
1991	2,158	1,515	1,527	295	96	5,591
1992	2,316	1,654	1,620	309	108	6,006
1993	2,320	1,717	1,631	303	111	6,081
1994	2,337	1,792	1,643	301	114	6,187
1995	2,291	1,779	1,584	293	114	6,061
1996	2,311	1,719	1,594	292	113	6,030
1997	2,250	1,615	1,490	293	117	5,765
1998	2,335	1,586	1,516	316	111	5,864
1999	2,443	1,603	1,789	303	102	6,239
2000	2,473	1,586	1,656	312	98	6,126
2001	2,585	1,623	1,652	318	107	6,285
2002	2,695	1,641	1,706	325	80	6,447
2003	2,799	1,617	1,749	329	64	6,558
2004	2,914	1,633	1,824	333	66	6,771
2005	2,982	1,655	1,832	316	68	6,853
2006	3,039	1,727	1,938	318	74	7,097
2007	3,186	1,832	2,401	335	83	7,838
2008	3,247	1,872	1,958	350	88	7,515
2009	3,413	1,947	2,036	360	93	7,849

Table 11

TABLE 11. PROVINCIAL GOVERNMENT EXPENDITURE ON TRANSPORTATION AND
COMMUNICATIONS PER CAPITA: ALBERTA AND THE OTHER PROVINCES (2009$)

Year	CA expenditure (000,000 $)	AB expenditure (000,000 $)	CA – AB expenditure (000,000 $)	Others real expenditure per capita ($)	AB real expenditure per capita ($)
1989	7,074	920	6,154	380	631
1990	8,028	966	7,062	410	614
1991	8,677	972	7,705	418	574
1992	8,461	816	7,645	405	467
1993	8,316	781	7,535	387	437
1994	7,545	691	6,854	348	376
1995	8,663	662	8,001	393	348
1996	8,713	618	8,095	388	313
1997	8,362	576	7,786	364	281
1998	8,028	672	7,356	338	316
1999	10,586	759	9,827	441	342
2000	9,486	1,215	8,271	358	520
2001	8,552	1,217	7,335	307	500
2002	8,755	1,309	7,446	302	508
2003	9,224	905	8,319	325	331
2004	9,606	1,077	8,529	325	381
2005	10,366	1,205	9,161	339	408
2006	13,367	2,003	11,364	409	633
2007	14,168	2,102	12,066	421	617
2008	16,802	3,093	13,709	462	861
2009	17,423	3,779	13,644	454	1,029

Alberta's spending in this area includes highways, water pipelines, transit and telecommunications. It has swung dramatically up and down. From $574 per person in 1989, it fell to under $350 from 1995 to 1999, as construction projects were delayed and maintenance deferred. It jumped by over thirty percent in 2000. Then, in 2003, it dropped back to the levels of 1999. From 2005 to 2009 it more than doubled, rising from $408 per person to $1,029, far above the rest of the country.

When the swings are averaged out, Alberta's spending on transportation and communication from 2000 to 2009 ranked fourth in the country.

TABLE 11A (OTHER SPENDING). PROVINCIAL GOVERNMENT EXPENDITURE ON
ENVIRONMENT PER CAPITA: ALBERTA AND THE OTHER PROVINCES (2009$)

Year	CA expenditure (000,000 $)	AB expenditure (000,000 $)	CA − AB expenditure (000,000 $)	Others real per capita ($)	AB real per capita ($)
1989	1,588	241	1,347	83	165
1990	1,882	275	1,607	93	175
1991	2,109	294	1,815	99	174
1992	2,188	230	1,958	104	132
1993	2,061	202	1,859	95	113
1994	1,911	193	1,718	87	105
1995	2,144	405	1,739	85	213
1996	2,080	301	1,779	85	153
1997	1,923	312	1,611	75	152
1998	1,707	287	1,420	65	135
1999	1,512	212	1,300	58	95
2000	1,681	273	1,408	61	117
2001	1,401	234	1,167	49	96
2002	1,525	223	1,302	53	87
2003	1,715	230	1,485	58	84
2004	1,646	214	1,432	55	76
2005	1,822	242	1,580	58	82
2006	2,009	479	1,530	55	151
2007	2,314	473	1,841	64	139
2008	2,506	593	1,913	65	165
2009	2,827	723	2,104	70	197

Spending on environmental services — such as pollution control, water
purification, sewage treatment, and environmental management — has
varied a lot, particularly in recent years. From 1991 to 1994 it dropped,
but unlike most other services it then climbed notably through the mid-
1990s. However, beginning in 1999 it began a marked decline, falling
from $135 per capita in 1998 to an average of $85 for the five years 2001
to 2005. Since then, spending has climbed.

Two things to note regarding Alberta's environmental spending:

- Despite the far larger economy and the rise of environmental
  concerns, Alberta spent almost precisely the same amount
  per person on the environment in the five years 2005–09
  (average: $144) as it did in the five years 1989–93 (average: $152).

- Compared to most other provinces, Alberta spends more on the environment. From 2000 to 2009, only P.E.I. and Newfoundland spent more. Alberta's generally higher spending in this area may come from the scale of environmental challenges posed by its petroleum industry.

TABLE 11B (OTHER SPENDING). PROVINCIAL GOVERNMENT EXPENDITURE ON RESOURCE CONSERVATION AND INDUSTRIAL DEVELOPMENT PER CAPITA: ALBERTA AND THE OTHER PROVINCES (2009$)

Year	CA expenditure (000,000 $)	AB expenditure (000,000 $)	CA – AB expenditure (000,000 $)	Others real resource conservation and industrial development expenditure per capita ($)	AB real resource conservation and industrial development expenditure per capita ($)
1989	7,478	1,775	5,703	352	1,218
1990	8,478	1,696	6,782	394	1,078
1991	7,975	1,614	6,361	345	953
1992	9,815	1,856	7,959	421	1,063
1993	9,349	2,142	7,207	370	1,199
1994	8,242	1,546	6,696	340	842
1995	7,284	1,139	6,145	302	599
1996	7,209	1,039	6,170	296	526
1997	6,954	885	6,069	284	431
1998	6,487	782	5,705	262	367
1999	7,868	948	6,920	310	427
2000	8,752	1,236	7,516	326	529
2001	8,922	1,174	7,748	324	482
2002	9,797	1,648	8,149	330	640
2003	11,459	2,426	9,033	353	887
2004	10,228	2,108	8,120	309	747
2005	10,288	1,972	8,316	307	667
2006	10,916	1,967	8,949	322	622
2007	11,709	2,047	9,662	337	601
2008	12,391	1,786	10,605	358	497
2009	12,547	2,464	10,083	336	671

Spending in this area covers such things as agriculture subsidies, support and incentives for the oil and gas industry, managing forestry, and promoting tourism. It reached highs of about $1,200 per capita in both 1989 and 1993. From 1996 to 2001 it fell to a much lower range, going as low as $367. Then, largely driven by costs associated with the BSE crisis in the beef industry, spending rose in 2003 and 2004, before returning to the more typical $600 range by 2006.

Alberta's spending in this area is consistently higher than the average of the other provinces.

TABLE 11C (OTHER SPENDING). PROVINCIAL GOVERNMENT EXPENDITURE ON PROTECTION OF PERSONS AND PROPERTY PER CAPITA: ALBERTA AND THE OTHER PROVINCES (2009$)

Year	CA expenditure (000,000 $)	AB expenditure (000,000 $)	CA – AB expenditure (000,000 $)	Others real per capita ($)	AB real per capita ($)
1989	4,801	454	4,347	268	311
1990	5,311	544	4,767	277	346
1991	5,928	495	5,433	295	292
1992	6,374	542	5,832	309	310
1993	6,432	543	5,889	303	304
1994	6,430	506	5,924	301	276
1995	6,385	433	5,952	293	228
1996	6,553	473	6,080	292	240
1997	6,808	542	6,266	293	264
1998	7,432	549	6,883	316	258
1999	7,302	544	6,758	303	245
2000	7,763	553	7,210	312	237
2001	8,167	569	7,598	318	234
2002	8,681	658	8,023	325	256
2003	9,041	621	8,420	329	227
2004	9,423	671	8,752	333	238
2005	9,370	826	8,544	316	279
2006	9,836	990	8,846	318	313
2007	10,607	992	9,615	335	291
2008	11,494	1,112	10,382	350	309
2009	12,093	1,270	10,823	360	346

This table presents Alberta's spending on services such as police, courts, corrections services and firefighting. Compared to most other areas, spending in this area has been fairly stable. During the past twenty years it has generally ranged between about $225 and $300 per person. In 2009, the spending level per capita was exactly the same as it was in 1990.

The same data on other provinces shows that Alberta ranked well below mid-range provinces such as Ontario and B.C., and distantly behind top-spending provinces such as Saskatchewan and Newfoundland.

Table 12

TABLE 12. TOTAL PROVINCIAL GOVERNMENT REVENUE PER CAPITA: ALBERTA AND THE OTHER PROVINCES (2009$)

Year	CA revenue (000,000 $)	AB revenue (000,000 $)	CA – AB revenue (000,000 $)	Others real revenue per capita ($)	AB real revenue per capita ($)
1989	134,104	13,200	120,904	7,463	9,054
1990	145,888	13,952	131,936	7,657	8,871
1991	154,781	15,790	138,991	7,547	9,321
1992	154,798	15,252	139,546	7,384	8,733
1993	159,212	15,603	143,609	7,377	8,732
1994	165,212	15,870	149,342	7,580	8,644
1995	174,925	17,867	157,058	7,720	9,395
1996	182,814	17,486	165,328	7,928	8,861
1997	183,264	19,019	164,245	7,677	9,269
1998	189,937	19,928	170,009	7,816	9,363
1999	199,796	19,161	180,635	8,104	8,626
2000	216,086	22,388	193,698	8,391	9,581
2001	238,130	30,600	207,530	8,682	12,573
2002	229,823	24,953	204,870	8,304	9,691
2003	239,046	27,086	211,960	8,289	9,902
2004	254,062	30,075	223,987	8,527	10,652
2005	278,992	32,773	246,219	9,102	11,088
2006	300,507	39,971	260,536	9,370	12,640
2007	319,397	42,429	276,968	9,660	12,448
2008	338,970	42,978	295,992	9,984	11,957
2009	341,582	43,253	298,329	9,928	11,783

With its much more prosperous economy, Alberta's per capita provincial government revenues have been consistently higher than the average in the rest of Canada — no surprise there. However, government revenues haven't grown at anywhere near the pace that Alberta's economy has.

The one major blip in the numbers — the 2001 spike in Alberta government revenues — was driven by a jump in natural gas royalties,

KEVIN TAFT   123 and the government's sale of "power purchase agreements" for electricity (part of its controversial deregulation of the electricity market). Revenues rose from an average of $8,942 for the five years form 1989–93 to an average of $11,983 for the five years from 2005–09. This 34 percent increase is much less than the growth of Alberta's economy.

TABLE 12A. ALBERTA GOVERNMENT EXPENDITURE AND REVENUE AS A PERCENTAGE OF GDP (2009$)

Year	AB nominal GDP (000,000 $)	AB total expenditure (000,000 $)	AB total revenues (000,000 $)	AB expenditure/ GDP (%)	AB revenues/ GDP (%)
1989	67,377	14,687	13,200	21.80%	19.59%
1990	73,257	15,933	13,952	21.75%	19.05%
1991	72,892	16,868	15,790	23.14%	21.66%
1992	74,936	17,375	15,252	23.19%	20.35%
1993	81,179	18,731	15,603	23.07%	19.22%
1994	88,041	18,337	15,870	20.83%	18.03%
1995	92,036	16,884	17,867	18.34%	19.41%
1996	98,634	16,230	17,486	16.45%	17.73%
1997	107,048	16,364	19,019	15.29%	17.77%
1998	107,439	17,016	19,928	15.84%	18.55%
1999	117,080	17,957	19,161	15.34%	16.37%
2000	144,789	19,704	22,388	13.61%	15.46%
2001	151,274	22,933	30,600	15.16%	20.23%
2002	150,594	25,785	24,953	17.12%	16.57%
2003	170,113	24,452	27,086	14.37%	15.92%
2004	189,743	25,683	30,075	13.54%	15.85%
2005	219,810	27,511	32,773	12.52%	14.91%
2006	238,886	31,150	39,971	13.04%	16.73%
2007	255,787	33,313	42,429	13.02%	16.59%
2008	291,577	38,294	42,978	13.13%	14.74%
2009	247,184	42,058	43,253	17.01%	17.50%

With the exception of 2001's jump in revenues, explained in the note for the previous table, Alberta's government has been collecting a progressively smaller portion of our province's economy.

Government revenues, which in 1991 reached a peak of 21.66 percent, dropped to a low of 14.7 percent in 2008. In 2009, government revenues rose as a portion of GDP because Alberta's GDP shrank during the global financial crisis of 2008–09.

Here are the numbers on government revenues in some other provinces for comparison:

- Ontario's government has collected a relatively consistent portion of its economy — in a range roughly from 16 to19 percent.

- Quebec has consistently collected a larger portion of its GDP than either Alberta or Ontario. But, like Ontario, its revenue has remained within a fairly narrow range, although significantly higher at 24 to 29 percent.

- Manitoba's government has collected an extremely stable percentage in recent decades — hovering around 25 percent.

- Saskatchewan's government has collected a significantly larger portion of its GDP than Alberta, consistently more than 21 percent, except 2008.

- British Columbia's provincial revenues have been very stable over the years, falling mostly between 20 and 23 percent.

Table 13

TABLE 13. VALUE OF THE HERITAGE FUND (2009$)

Year	Nominal value Heritage Fund ($)	Real value Heritage Fund ($)
1977	1,162	4,040
1978	1,664	5,315
1979	2,204	6,442
1980	2,687	7,192
1981	3,470	8,242
1982	4,266	9,089
1983	4,970	9,871
1984	5,116	9,720
1985	5,294	9,703
1986	5,401	9,487
1987	5,381	9,087
1988	5,269	8,533
1989	5,138	7,958
1990	4,975	7,318
1991	4,844	6,710
1992	4,978	6,788
1993	5,057	6,767
1994	4,798	6,405
1995	4,734	6,189
1996	4,797	6,179
1997	4,467	5,645
1998	4,749	5,943
1999	4,509	5,588
2000	4,464	5,368
2001	4,169	4,895
2002	4,146	4779
2003	3,650	4,036
2004	4,043	4,436
2005	3,841	4,119
2006	4,570	4,797
2007	4,943	5,072
2008	4,965	5,027
2009	3,899	3,900

The data for this table came from Alberta Finance and Enterprise.

The average value of the Heritage Fund per capita (2009$) for the five-year period 1989–93 was $7,108, and for the five-year period 2005–09 was $4,583.

This is a drop in value of $2,525, or 35 percent.

Table 14

TABLE 14. PERSONAL INCOME AND TAX PER CAPITA: ALBERTA (2009$)

Year	AB personal income (000,000 $)	AB personal income taxes (000,000 $)	AB personal income per capita ($)	AB personal income taxes per capita ($)
1989	50,377	2,040	34,555	1,399
1990	55,010	2,539	34,978	1,614
1991	57,519	2,797	33,953	1,651
1992	58,975	3,058	33,769	1,751
1993	61,013	2,794	34,143	1,564
1994	62,088	3,008	33,818	1,638
1995	64,528	3,063	33,930	1,611
1996	66,938	3,177	33,920	1,610
1997	72,952	3,446	35,553	1,679
1998	78,279	3,876	36,779	1,821
1999	81,151	4,600	36,535	2,071
2000	89,094	5,122	38,130	2,192
2001	98,131	4,320	40,320	1,775
2002	101,072	4,537	39,255	1,762
2003	105,664	4,877	38,629	1,783
2004	115,269	4,658	40,824	1,650
2005	128,285	4,699	43,401	1,590
2006	146,058	4,728	46,189	1,495
2007	160,149	7,673	46,984	2,251
2008	172,209	8,322	47,911	2,315
2009	171,342	8,666	46,678	2,361

The five-year average (2009$) for 1989–93 for personal incomes per capita was $34,280, and for 2005–09 was $46,233 — a 34 percent growth in Alberta's personal incomes over the last twenty-one years. The same calculation for Alberta's GDP per capita shows that Alberta's economy grew about 67 percent over the same time period.

The table below highlights how consistently low Alberta's personal income taxes have been in recent decades. As a portion of overall income, they have remained below the average for the rest of Canada — often far below — throughout the years reflected in this table.

TABLE 14A. PERSONAL INCOME TAX AS A PERCENTAGE OF INCOME: ALBERTA AND THE OTHER PROVINCES (2009$)

Year	AB personal income (000,000 $)	CA personal income (000,000 $)	Others personal income (000,000 $)	AB personal income taxes (000,000 $)	CA personal income taxes (000,000 $)	Others personal income taxes (000,000 $)	Others % tax paid on income	AB % tax paid on income
1989	50,377	546,324	495,947	2,040	31,099	29,059	5.86%	4.05%
1990	55,010	586,566	531,556	2,539	34,622	32,083	6.04%	4.62%
1991	57,519	605,322	547,803	2,797	39,320	36,523	6.67%	4.86%
1992	58,975	620,653	561,678	3,058	38,623	35,565	6.33%	5.19%
1993	61,013	633,059	572,046	2,794	37,494	34,700	6.07%	4.58%
1994	62,088	646,348	584,260	3,008	40,566	37,558	6.43%	4.84%
1995	64,528	672,111	607,583	3,063	40,486	37,423	6.16%	4.75%
1996	66,938	687,203	620,265	3,177	43,264	40,087	6.46%	4.75%
1997	72,952	715,495	642,543	3,446	45,229	41,783	6.50%	4.72%
1998	78,279	748,321	670,042	3,876	46,890	43,014	6.42%	4.95%
1999	81,151	783,060	701,909	4,600	49,504	44,904	6.40%	5.67%
2000	89,094	840,382	751,288	5,122	53,006	47,884	6.37%	5.75%
2001	98,131	876,471	778,340	4,320	53,933	49,613	6.37%	4.40%
2002	101,072	898,843	797,771	4,537	53,311	48,774	6.11%	4.49%
2003	105,664	931,773	826,109	4,877	51,465	46,588	5.64%	4.62%
2004	115,269	984,164	868,895	4,658	52,611	47,953	5.52%	4.04%
2005	128,285	1,035,586	907,301	4,699	56,782	52,083	5.74%	3.66%
2006	146,058	1,106,832	960,774	4,728	61,713	56,985	5.93%	3.24%
2007	160,149	1,174,683	1,014,534	7,673	71,731	64,058	6.31%	4.79%
2008	172,209	1,224,653	1,052,444	8,322	75,134	66,812	6.35%	4.83%
2009	171,342	1,228,407	1,057,065	8,666	74,901	66,235	6.27%	5.06%

Table 15

TABLE 15. ALBERTA CORPORATE INCOME AND TAX PER CAPITA (2009$)

Year	AB corporation profits before taxes (000,000 $)	AB corporation income taxes (000,000 $)	AB corporation profits before taxes per capita ($)	AB corporation income taxes per capita ($)
1989	6,439	544	4,417	373
1990	6,857	648	4,360	412
1991	4,674	803	2,759	474
1992	4,604	730	2,636	418
1993	6,406	633	3,585	354
1994	10,769	833	5,866	454
1995	12,431	1,061	6,536	558
1996	14,571	1,319	7,384	668
1997	15,604	1,396	7,605	680
1998	11,670	1,835	5,483	862
1999	16,236	1,649	7,310	742
2000	30,206	1,229	12,927	526
2001	28,909	2,000	11,878	822
2002	23,229	2,215	9,022	860
2003	32,944	1,989	12,044	727
2004	40,750	1,666	14,432	590
2005	51,294	2,337	17,354	791
2006	50,182	2,889	15,869	914
2007	49,929	3,579	14,648	1,050
2008	66,501	4,695	18,502	1,306
2009	28,251	3,774	7,696	1,028

The five-year average for corporate income per capita in Alberta for 1989–93 is $3,551, and for 2005–09 is $14,814. This represents an increase of 317 percent in corporate income over twenty-one years.

TABLE 15A. CORPORATE INCOME PER CAPITA: ALBERTA AND THE
OTHER PROVINCES (2009$)

Year	AB corporation profits before taxes (000,000 $)	CA corporation profits before taxes (000,000 $)	Others corporation profits before taxes (000,000 $)	AB corporate profits per capita ($)	Others corporate profits per capita ($)
1989	6,439	59,661	53,222	4,417	3,285
1990	6,857	44,936	38,079	4,360	2,210
1991	4,674	32,920	28,246	2,759	1,534
1992	4,604	32,648	28,044	2,636	1,484
1993	6,406	41,102	34,696	3,585	1,782
1994	10,769	65,464	54,695	5,866	2,776
1995	12,431	76,270	63,839	6,536	3,138
1996	14,571	80,335	65,764	7,384	3,154
1997	15,604	87,932	72,328	7,605	3,380
1998	11,670	86,132	74,462	5,483	3,423
1999	16,236	110,769	94,533	7,310	4,241
2000	30,206	135,978	105,772	12,927	4,582
2001	28,909	127,073	98,164	11,878	4,107
2002	23,229	135,229	112,000	9,022	4,539
2003	32,944	144,501	111,557	12,044	4,363
2004	40,750	168,219	127,469	14,432	4,853
2005	51,294	186,585	135,291	17,354	5,001
2006	50,182	197,286	147,104	15,869	5,291
2007	49,929	200,943	151,014	14,648	5,267
2008	66,501	216,970	150,469	18,502	5,075
2009	28,251	146,897	118,646	7,696	3,948

Corporate profits in Alberta have been consistently higher than in
Canada's other provinces. In 2008, measured per capita, corporate
profits in Alberta were more than three times higher than in the other
provinces.

TABLE 15B. ROYALTIES PER CAPITA: ALBERTA AND THE
OTHER PROVINCES (2009$)

Year	CA royalties (000,000 $)	AB royalties (000,000 $)	CA – AB royalties (000,000 $)	Others real royalties per capita ($)	AB real royalties per capita ($)
1989	4,009	2,162	1,847	114	1,483
1990	4,565	2,687	1,878	109	1,709
1991	4,056	2,260	1,796	98	1,334
1992	4,024	2,218	1,806	96	1,270
1993	5,096	2,681	2,415	124	1,500
1994	6,892	3,476	3,416	173	1,893
1995	6,320	2,888	3,432	169	1,519
1996	7,398	3,586	3,812	183	1,817
1997	7,263	3,874	3,389	158	1,888
1998	6,823	2,876	3,947	181	1,351
1999	7,604	3,885	3,719	167	1,749
2000	14,134	8,867	5,267	228	3,795
2001	13,311	8,643	4,668	195	3,551
2002	10,372	5,786	4,586	186	2,247
2003	13,327	8,423	4,904	192	3,079
2004	14,668	9,315	5,353	204	3,299
2005	19,035	12,842	6,193	229	4,345
2006	19,534	13,628	5,906	212	4,310
2007	17,163	10,925	6,238	218	3,205
2008	23,068	14,023	9,045	305	3,901

The CANSIM data available for this table ended in 2008.

Alberta's oil and gas royalties set it apart from all other provinces. Alberta usually earns more in royalties than all the rest of Canada combined. Only three other provinces (B.C., Saskatchewan and Newfoundland) receive notable revenues from royalties, and their totals come nowhere near Alberta's. For the remaining six provinces, royalty revenues are very small. From 2000 to 2008 (the most up-to-date year available for this Statistics Canada data), Ontario averaged $23 per person a year, and Quebec $33, compared to an average of $3,526 in Alberta.

Royalties are often Alberta's largest single source of provincial income. In recent years, royalties have exceeded corporate and personal income taxes combined.

From 1989 to 1999, Alberta's royalties stayed in the range of $1,270 to $1,893 per person per year. With the surge in natural gas prices in 2000, royalties jumped dramatically, hitting $3,795 per person in 2000 and $3,551 in 2001. Royalty revenue then eased down with lower natural gas prices, until spiking again in 2005 and 2006, as both oil and natural gas prices soared once again. (This data includes earnings from oil and gas land rights auctions.)

From 2003 to 2008, Alberta's royalties per capita averaged $3,690 each year. The average for the rest of Canada was $227. This is the real Alberta advantage, but it comes from a non-renewable resource — and the world is increasingly working to reduce its dependence on hydrocarbons.

About the Authors

Kevin Taft has spent most of his career working on public policy in government, in the non-profit sector, and in private practice. He has published three other books on Alberta politics and policy: *Shredding the Public Interest*; *Clear Answers: The Economics and Politics of For-Profit Medicine* (co-authored with Gillian Steward); and *Democracy Derailed*. He served three terms as an MLA in the Alberta Legislature, including almost five years as leader of the Opposition. He has a Ph.D. in business.

Melville McMillan is a professor in the Department of Economics, and a fellow of the Institute of Public Economics, at the University of Alberta. His B.A. and M.Sc. are from the University of Alberta, and his Ph.D. is from Cornell University. McMillan's research and teaching interests are in public economics and public finance, and he has taught, published and advised — nationally and internationally — in these areas.

Junaid Jahangir completed a Ph.D. in economics at the University of Alberta in 2011. His dissertation explored the impact of electricity market restructuring on residential consumers in Alberta. He is a full-time lecturer in economics at Grant MacEwan University.